Making Classic Chairs

A Craftsman's Chippendale Reference

By Ron Clarkson

With A Special Historical Notes Chapter
By Leigh Keno
Leigh Keno American Antiques, New York

Collection Development Information

FOX BOOKS
Fox Chapel Publishing Co Inc.

Box 7948
Lancaster, PA 17604

Manufactured in the United States of America

ISBN #1–56523–081–7

Publisher: Alan Giagnocavo
Project Editor: Ayleen Stellhorn
Design: Charles Golding
Photography: Richard Hertzler

Additional Photography: Bob Polett/VMI Productions, Leola, PA
                            Museum of Fine Arts, Boston
                            Leigh Keno American Antiques, New York, NY

Cover Design: Robert Altland, Altland Design

To order a copy of this book
please send cover price plus $2.50:

FOX CHAPEL PUBLISHING, Book Orders
Box 7948
Lancaster, PA 17604

Please try your favorite book supplier first!

Our special thanks to: Leigh Keno American Antiques, New York
                           Museum of Fine Arts, Boston

DEDICATION

In memory of my father, Lewis "Jack" Clarkson, and my mentor, Robert Eastburn.

DISCLAIMER

The projects in this book require the use of power tools which are, by nature, inherently dangerous to work with. It is very important that you follow basic common sense as well as manufacturer's manuals and operating procedures for the equipment shown in these pages.

Due to the educational focus of this book, the author may have removed standard safeguards or other safety items in order to illustrate techniques.

Ron Clarkson and Fox Chapel Publishing can assume no liability if you operate machinery outside recommended safety guidelines.

Be careful, be safe and enjoy woodworking for years to come!

ACKNOWLEDGEMENTS

I would like to thank the following people for their encouragement and support of this project:

Jody Garrett and Woodcraft Supply Corporation of Parkersburg, W. Va.
DeWalt Tool Company
Wagner Spray Tech Company
CMT Tool Company
JET Power Tools
Veritas Tools

and Richard Hertzler for his patience during the long hours of photography sessions.

Contents

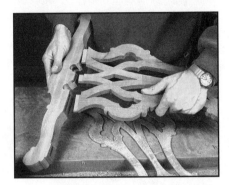

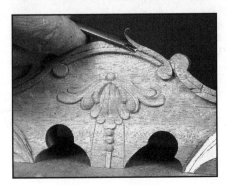

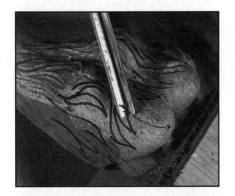

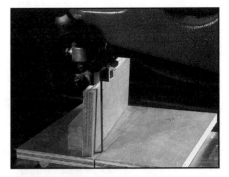

PUBLISHER'S INTRODUCTION

Reproducing period furniture is currently experiencing a resurgence among craftsmen today. There is a renewed interest in the lines and classic styles of furniture made in a period when committed craftsmanship was an accepted rule and not the exception that it has become in today's industrialized society.

One of the problems an interested craftsman has in regaining the knowledge necessary to build quality, authentic pieces is the lack of teachers and publications. This volume will serve to partially fill this void. Because much of this expertise was originally passed on through the apprentice system, we felt it only appropriate to devote much of the book to an in-depth look at the progression of a Chippendale style chair from start to finish.

As you refer to these 400 photos, you'll have the same advantages that an apprentice of the 1700s had in watching every aspect of design and construction.

But we are never satisfied to publish just a "how-to" book! So in the front and back sections of this book you'll benefit from much "why-to" information. This will lead you to a solid understanding of the history and finer design points of the projects you are undertaking. We are especially grateful to Leigh Keno, an expert in antique American furniture, for his contribution on appreciating Chippendale styles and history.

As you admire Ron Clarkson's craftsmanship, I hope this will bring out your own creativity and talent. Then we will have been truly successful with this book.

J. Alan Giagnocavo
Publisher

CHAPTER ONE

Chippendale Furniture and the Philadelphia Style

by Leigh Keno
Leigh Keno American Antiques, New York

Its fine appearance, good regulations, agreeable situation, natural advantages, trade, riches and power, are by no means inferior to those of any, even of the most ancient towns in Europe.[1]

So wrote the Swedish naturalist Peter Kalm, following his 1748 visit to Philadelphia. In fact, what Kalm had observed was just the beginning of the city's rise to a position of economic prominence in the American colonies. Situated at the juncture of the Schuykill and Delaware Rivers, Philadelphia's economic sphere had broadened significantly towards the end of the 1750s as the city's merchants tapped the lush countryside for tradable goods. Wheat, flour, barreled meats, lumber, limestone, bricks, and flaxseed, all offered lucrative prospects for the Pennsylvania traders. By mid-century Philadelphia held advantage over the ports of New York, Newport and Boston, because its closeness to the broadening network of western land routes increased accessibility to the hinterland. Between 1743 and 1760, the city's population expanded from 13,000 to 23,750. By comparison the populations of New York and Newport had only reached 18,000 and 7,500 respectively. Meanwhile at Boston, a town which had seen its economic heyday during the second quarter of the eighteenth-

[1] Peter Kalm, *Travels in North America* (1753 1761), trans, Adolph B. Benson (1770: reprint, New York: Wilson-Erickson, 1937), p. 24.

century, the population had actually declined from 16,382 to 15,631.[2]

"The Arts delight to travel westward," noted Benjamin Franklin to Polly Stevenson in 1763. "After the first cares for the necessities of life are over, we shall come to think of the embellishments...."[3] Inspired by the rococo splendor that had first hit Georgian England during the 1730s and '40s, America's colonial aristocracy looked to English prototypes to inspire locally made furniture fashions. In Philadelphia, where the economy was booming, immigrant and local craftsmen "found a monied and culturally aware citizenry awaiting the best and latest that their skills could produce."[4]

Fashion news reached American shores in the form of printed material, pattern books, imported objects, or in the hands-on experience of immigrant craftsmen. Shells, scrollwork, acanthus leaves and other foliate designs were some of the most popular rococo motifs, and by the 1740s they had begun to appear in architectural interiors as well as on engravings, silver and furnishings. At first, these decorative motifs were simply applied to objects that owed their form to the earlier traditions of Queen Anne style. In terms of seating furniture, the Queen Anne style was ideally characterized by a baroque sensibility defined by sensuous S-curves and C-scrolls and punctuated by small areas of natural ornament. The advent of rococo designs saw such contained areas of carved ornament evolve into larger expressions of pattern that dominated the form.

The London publication of Thomas Chippendale's comprehensive book of furniture designs, *The Gentleman & Cabinet-Maker's Director* (1754), further whet the colonial appetite for furniture in the rococo manner. Chippendale, a London-based merchant-craftsman, intended the book to be used as a reference tool of the latest English furniture designs for clients and for other craftsmen. Two subsequent editions (1755 and 1762) of *The Director,* clarified the tone of its designs, "Being a large collection of the most Elegant and Useful Designs of Household Furniture in Gothic, Chinese and Modern Taste."[5]

According to Chippendale, armed with a basic understanding of classical design theory, a craftsman could update his furniture productions using an overlay of the above-mentioned themes and motifs. Although many of the patterns put forth by the London merchant were not of Chippendale's own invention, and other design manuals such as Mattias Lock's *A New Book of Ornaments* (1752), Thomas Johnson's *A New Book of Ornaments* (1760), Ince and Mayhew's *The Universal System of Household Furniture* (1760), and Robert Manwaring's *The Cabinet and Chair-Maker's Real Friend and*

[2] Carl Bridenbaugh, *Cities in Revolt: Urban Life in America, 1743-1776* (New York, Alfred A. Knopf, Inc., 1955), p. 5.

[3] Carl and Jessica Bridenbaugh, *Rebels and Gentlemen: Philadelphia in the Age of Franklin* (New York: Reynal & Hitchcock, 1942), p. 135.

[4] Joan Barzilay Freund, *Masterpieces of Americana: The Collection of Mr. and Mrs. Adolph Henry Meyer* (New York: Sotheby's Books, 1995), p. 44.

[5] William M. Hornor, Jr., *Blue Book: Philadelphia Furniture* (1935; reprint, Washington, D.C.: Highland House, 1977), p. 70.

Companion (1765), were published during the same time period, Chippendale's sound marketing skills caused his name to be inextricably linked to the rococo designs that characterized the era.

Concurrent with the progress of style was a deepening resentment and nervousness on the part of American tradesmen and their patrons of the restrictive economic policies handed down by the British Board of Trade. "Household goods may be had here as cheap and as well made from English patterns," cautioned Philadelphia's Samuel Morris to his nephew, Samuel Powel, Jr. in London. "In the humour people are in here, a man is in danger of becoming Invidiously distinguished, who buys anything in England which our Tradesmen can furnish. I have heard the joiners here object this against Dr. Morgan & other who brought their furnishings with them..."[6] Eventually, the growing public sentiment for the boycott of British goods was codified in various nonimportation agreements signed in Boston and New York in 1768-70 and in Philadelphia in 1769-70. These agreements were a boon to local craftsmen like upholsterer Plunkett Fleeson, cabinetmaker James James, turner Jacob Shoemaker, Jr., chairmaker Joseph Trotter and carvers Hercules Courtenay, Martin Jugiez, and Nicholas Bernard, all of whom signed the Pennsylvania Resolutions.[7]

"Manufactures, when they are in perfection, are carried on by a multiplicity of hands, each of which is expert only in his own part, no one of them a master of the whole." This observation by Benjamin Franklin, well characterizes the advantages of an urban-based furniture shop tradition. Most often, complex furniture designs, particularly the highly ornate patterns of the Rococo, represent the collaborative effort of several craft specialists such as a designer, a joiner and a carver. Seating furniture was no exception.

On November 25, 1762, one remarkable team of carvers introduced themselves to the Philadelphia public:

> *...BERNARD and JUGIEZ Carvers and Gilders, at their Looking-Glass Store, in Walnut-Street, between Front and Second-streets...A compleat assortment of Looking-Glasses, framed in the newest Taste, Picture Frames, Sconces, Chimney Pieces, Ornaments for Ceilings, Pictures Framed and Glazed, a neat Harpsichord. N.B. All Sort of Carving in Wood or Stone and Gilding done in the neatest Manner."[8]*

Nicholas Bernard and Martin Jugiez were a pair of craftsmen who, as described in the advertisement, practiced both architectural and furniture carving. Their partnership is thought to have extended from 1762 to 1783. A number of still extant bills and receipts prove that they provided the

[6] Hornor, p. 81.
[7] Hornor, p. 80.
[8] *The Arts and Crafts in Philadelphia, Maryland and South Carolina*, coll., Alfred Coxe Prime (Philadelphia: The Walpole Society, 1929), p. 202 3.

carved ornament for furniture made by other local craftsmen such as the Scottish-born Thomas Affleck and the American-born cabinetmakers, James Gillingham and Benjamin Randolph.

In a 1985 article for *The Magazine Antiques,* furniture historian Luke Beckerdite used examples of architectural carving attributable to Bernard and Jugiez as a touchstone for identifying examples of their furniture carving. Beckerdite made his case using design details that appeared in the interiors of a number of significant Philadelphia-area structures such as Cliveden, the mansion of Chief Justice, Benjamin Chew (1763-1767), the pulpit wall of Saint Peter's Church, Philadelphia (1758-1763), and the interiors of Captain John Macpherson's Mount Pleasant home (1761-1765).

The carving of a magnificent, circa 1765, scroll-foot side chair shown in Figure 1 can be attributed based largely upon Beckerdite's findings to Bernard and Jugiez. The chair is the only known Philadelphia chair that aims to completely replicate a design based upon Chippendale's *Director.* Both the splat and feet of the chair are derived directly from Plate 12 of the 1754 edition (Fig. 2). In execution this chair presents the quintessence of rococo design displayed on an American-made chair.

The chair's serpentine crest rail is headed by acanthus scrolls and bell flowers centering an openwork cartouche and ending with flourished, ruffled ears. The molded stiles flank a pierced splat that incorporates an attenuated lozenge with a Chinese-inspired X-motif. This same motif appears on the lower shaft between the juncture of the legs of a well-known pie-crust tea table formerly in the collection of Eddy Nicholson.[9] The lower part of the splat features a highly ornate, decorated open cartouche with ruffles and C-scrolls offset by flanking leafage. Each of the chair's boldly fashioned front legs could stand alone as a piece of sculpture. The robustly carved knees display acanthus-carved strapwork flanked by C-scroll, leafy brackets. The entire leg form then sweeps sumptuously downward to form a scrolled foot with an open center carved from the solid.

The use of deeply incised gadrooning on all three sides of the seat rail is a rarity in Philadelphia design, which may have been inspired by the carver's need to balance the gutsy execution of the leg design. Other details reveal the stylistic lexicon of Bernard and Jugiez. The lobes of the acanthus leaves that rise off the feet are deeply outlined on the leg sides with veined flutes used to visually elongate the tips of each leaf. The same modeled effect was used by the carvers to define the leaves on the consoles over the door in the first floor drawing room at Cliveden, the keystones on the pulpit wall of Saint Peter's Church, and the chimney-piece consoles,

[9] *The Collection of Mr. and Mrs. Eddy Nicholson,* (Christie's New York, January 28, 1995), lot 1081.

fashioned for the first-floor drawing room of Mount Pleasant.[10]

As Beckerdite observed, the chair's carving was executed with the type of hearty vigor ordinarily reserved for architectural rather than furniture work. The applied gadrooning, the deeply incised scrolls and leaves on the feet, the vigorous design of the crest rail and knee carving are all heavy-handed. He drew further comparison between the attenuated shape of the leaves cascading from the chair's C-scrolled knees, to the foliate detail that appears on the keystones and cupboards of John Macpherson's second-floor drawing room. In both instances, the same vertical gouge cuts were used to define the shape of each attenuated leaf. A four-point punch used to fill the relieved void of the knees was a favorite ploy of Bernard and Jugiez. Similar work can be found on the legs of a dressing table attributed to the carvers, which is now at the Museum of Early Southern Decorative Arts.[11]

In its sense of verticality and proportion, the chair maintains a distinctly American feel. Regional construction preference such as the slightly raked rear stump legs, the side rails tenoned through the rear stiles, and the use of northern white cedar glue blocks confirm its Philadelphia heritage.

Another side chair, from a set of at least four, also features carving attributable to Bernard and Jugiez (Fig. 3). This example features an acanthus and C-scroll carved, shaped crest rail extending out to shell carved terminals, above a pierced acanthus and C-scroll carved, Gothic vase-form splat centering an X-carved reserve. The molded seat rail enclosing the slip seat is supported by flowerhead and acanthus-carved cabriole legs ending in claw and ball feet.

As with the previous example, the chair in Figure 3 is stylistically derived from Plate 12 of the 1754 Director. In this instance a traditional Philadelphia cabriole leg ending in webbed, slightly raked claw and ball feet with well articulated, crisply carved talons and subtle depressions between the knuckles has been substituted for the scroll foot. The design of the cartouche in the lower part of the splat was also simplified and lacks the ruffled edge seen on the scroll foot example. Chippendale recognized that both the size of a patron's pocketbook and the level of a craftsman's expertise varied, and he supportively noted in his text, "if any of the small Ornaments should be thought superfluous, they may be left out, without spoiling the Design."[12]

A third chair now at the Museum of Fine Arts, Boston, also dates to circa 1765.[13] It presents a superb example of a Philadelphia scrolled-strapwork splat (Fig. 4). This classic chair also features a crest rail with acanthus leaves that extend from the outermost lobes of the central shell to form the top of its serpentine edge. All the chair's ornamentation is vigorously carved in crisp high relief, from the architecturally inspired,

[10] The work done at Clivedon in Germantown, Pa., represents the earliest work documented to the team. On March 30, 1766 they were paid "L7/18 for carving two 'troles' (or consoles), at thirteen shillings each, ten smaller consoles and fourteen feet of 'egg-and-tongue' molding valued at three shillings per foot." The bill is listed under "Cliveden-Building Materials-Repairs" in the *Chew Family Papers* (Historical Society of Pennsylvania, Philadelphia, as noted by Luke Beckerdite in "Philadelphia Carving Shops," Part II, "Bernard and Jugiez," *The Magazine Antiques* (September 1985), pp 498-513.

[11] Luke Beckerdite, p. 507, figs. 19 and 19a.

[12] *American Art: 1750 1800, Toward Independence*, eds. Charles F. Montgomery and Patricia E. Kane (Boston: New York Graphic Society), p. 155.

[13] John T. Kirk, *American Chairs: Queen Anne and Chippendale* (New York: Alfred A. Knopf, 1972), p. 81, fig. 72.

stop fluted stiles to the deeply gadrooned shoe, to the stylized tassel that hangs in the splat's central void.

The paired S-scrolls of the splat flanking the chord and tassel recall only slightly Plate 14 of the 1762 edition of *The Director.* Yet, the design seems to reject the lighter asymmetry favored by Chippendale in favor of a more self-contained gesture. The stop-fluted stiles with strong, outwardly scrolled ears, the matched symmetry of the shell on the crest and front seat rail, and even the depth of the seat rail are all slightly reminiscent of earlier Georgian chairs. Such modifications were no doubt client specified by folks seeking a more tempered elegance.

Three virtually identical sets of chairs with carved strapwork backs and carved pendant tassels are known. Chairs from these sets vary primarily in differentials of height and in the number of lobes assigned to the front rail shells.[14] Tradition maintains an armchair (which is probably missing the carved cord and tassel motif in its central elliptical void) that descended in the family of Philadelphia cabinetmaker, Jonathan Shoemaker (1726-1793) was crafted by him.[15] The chair's carving is believed to be from the same shop that generated a Philadelphia high chest and tea table now in the Diplomatic reception room of the U.S. Department of State. Similar carving can be found on a high chest and matching dressing table and the base of another high chest all in the Garvan Collection at Yale University.[16] To date, the name of the carver has remained elusive, however the design vocabulary promoted by his shop is identifiable. He usually fashioned leaves that flip quickly at the tip and shaded the ends with deeply incised parallel chisel strokes. We are fortunate that over two centuries later we are able to recognize and appreciate the subtleties of this craftsman's genius.

— *Leigh Keno*

[14] Others are located in the Diplomatic Reception Rooms at the U.S. Department of State (see Clement E. Conger and Alexandra W. Rollins, *Treasures of State: Fine and Decorative Arts in the Diplomatic Reception Rooms of the U.S. Department of State* [New York: Harry N. Abrams, Inc., 1991], p. 105, pl. 23) and at the Henry Ford Museum. Chairs from two related sets are at the Winterthur Museum (see Joseph Downs, *American Furniture Queen Anne and Chippendale Periods in the Henry Francis du Pont Winterthur Museum* [New York: Macmillan Co., 1952], pl. 125) and at the Metropolitan Museum of Art (see Morrison Heckscher, *American Furniture in the Metropolitan Museum of Art, Late Colonial Period* [New York: Random House, 1985], no. 50).

[15] *Philadelphia, Three Centuries of American Art, Bicentennial Exhibition April 11 October 19, 1976* (Philadelphia: Philadelphia Museum of Art, 1976), no. 66.

[16] Luke Beckerdite and Alan Miller believe this all to have stemmed from the shop of one carver. See, Conger and Rollins, nos. 84 and 85.

FIGURE 1

CHIPPENDALE MAHOGANY SCROLL-FOOT SIDE CHAIR, carving attributed to the shop of Nicholas Bernard and Martin Jugiez, Philadelphia, circa 1765. (Courtesy of Leigh Keno)

Height:	39 3/4"
Width (at knee):	25 1/2"
Depth (at seat):	20 1/2"

FIGURE 2

PLATE 12 from the 1754 Edition of the *Director*, upon which the chair in Figure 1 is based.

FIGURE 3

CHIPPENDALE MAHOGANY SIDE CHAIR, carving attributed to the shop of Nicholas Bernard and Martin Jugiez, Philadelphia, circa 1765. (Courtesy of Leigh Keno)

Height: 40"
Width (at knee):   24 1/2"
Depth (at feet):   23 1/2"

FIGURE 4

Side chair, Philadelphia, 1755-95. Courtesy of Museum of Fine Arts, Boston. Gift of Mr. and Mrs. Maxim Karolik Collection.

PRIMARY WOOD: mahogany. SECONDARY WOOD: pine corner blocks and slip seat frame.
DIMENSION: height, 39 3/8 inches; width, 24 1/2; height of seat rail, 16 7/8.
DESIGN AND CONSTRUCTION: Back, bowed. Seat frame construction, as fig. 19. Bracing of seat frame, corner blocks, as fig. 19. Knee brackets, nailed. No bracket responds, but rear of side horizontal shaping cut to reverse curve. Horizontal shaping. Through tenons. Seating of splat in shoe.

CHAPTER TWO

Chippendale Style Reference

No history of American furniture would be complete without mention of Thomas Chippendale, the English-born cabinet maker who published *The Gentleman and Cabinet-Maker's Director* in 1754.

Little is known of Chippendale's life up until he published the *Director* at age 36. It is believed that he may have lived in a small village called Otley in Yorkshire, England, though some authorities write that he hailed from London. Likewise, little is known about his parents, except that his father may have been a cabinet maker as well.

Most likely, Chippendale's early years followed those of other young men studying to become master craftsmen under the guild system in place in England during the 18th century. He probably had little formal schooling and spent years learning the mysteries and secrets of his chosen trade as an apprentice and, later, as a journeyman.

Chippendale married in London around age 36 and fathered 11 children. Later in life, at 52, five years after the death of his first wife, he married again. At the time of the publication of the *Director* in 1754, his place of establishment was located along St. Martin's Lane in London and consisted of three houses. His business was successful and grew; at one point he had at least 22 journeyman cabinet makers and an untold number of apprentices.

Thomas Chippendale lived to be 61. He died from tuberculosis in 1779. His eldest son, Thomas, took over the business, continuing in his father's stead for 40-odd years until his death in 1822 or 1823.

On the following pages, you'll find information reprinted directly from Thomas Chippendale's *Director*. The book, first printed in 1754, had two subsequent editions in 1755 and 1762.

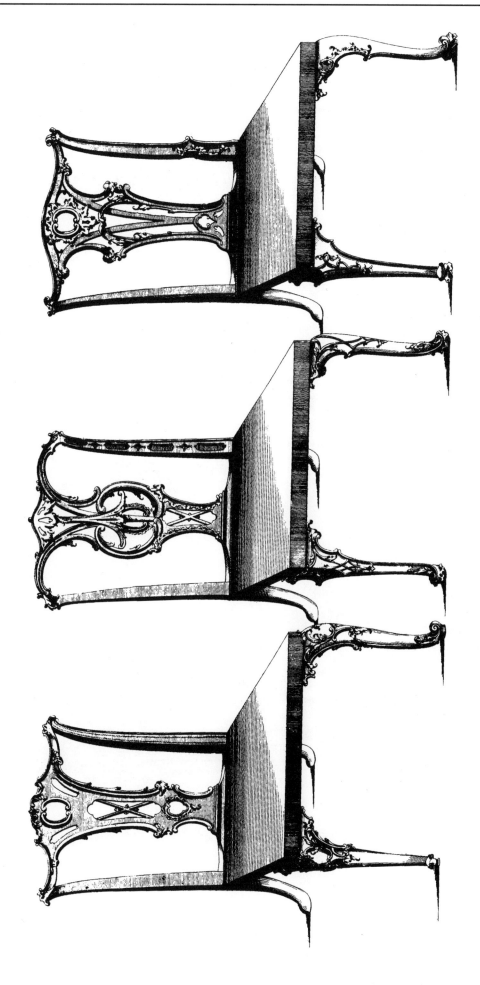

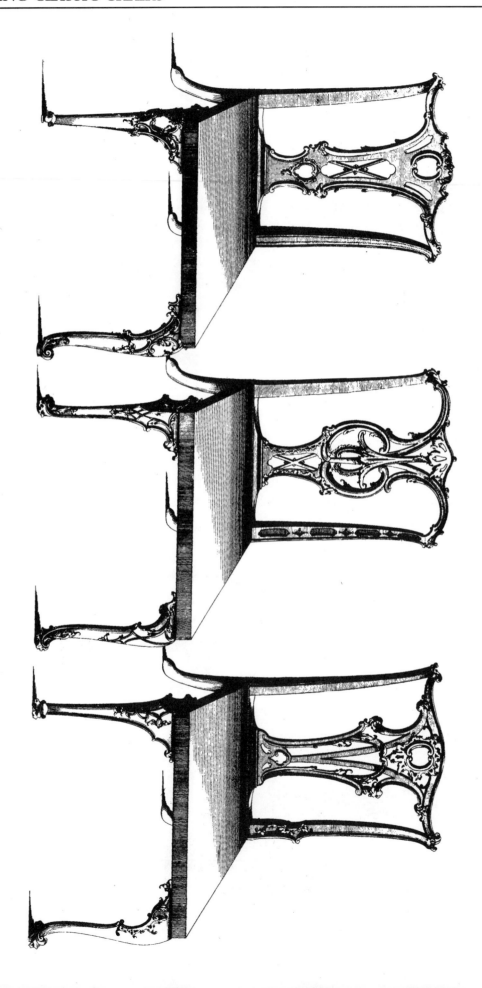

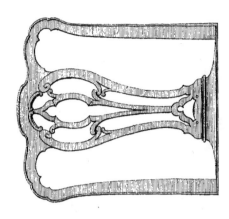

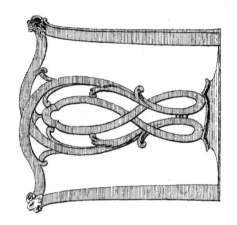

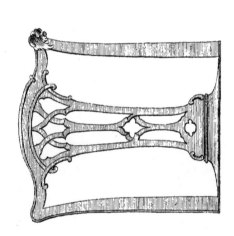

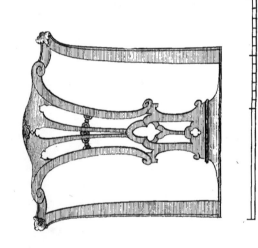

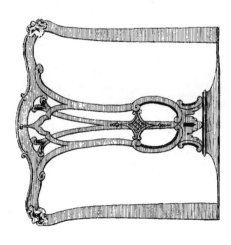

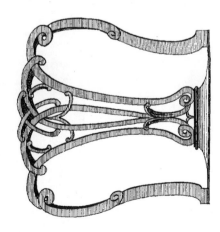

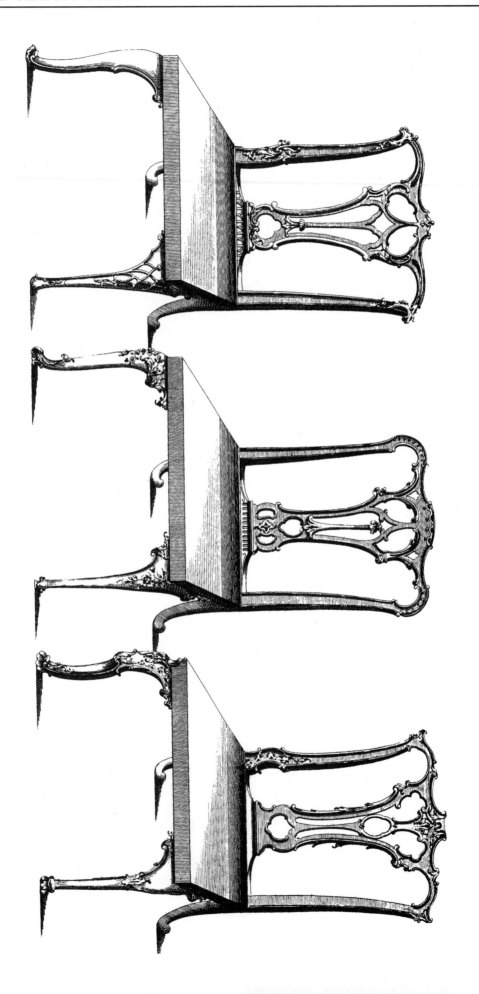

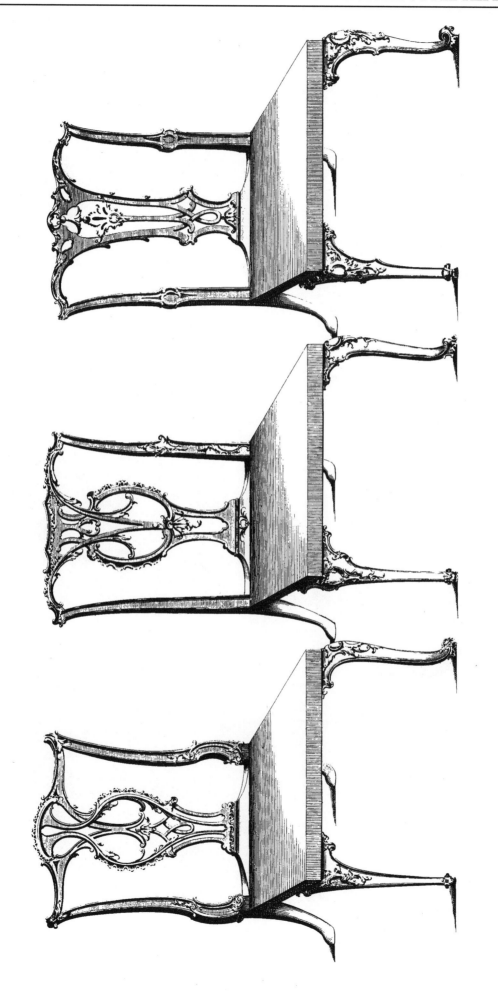

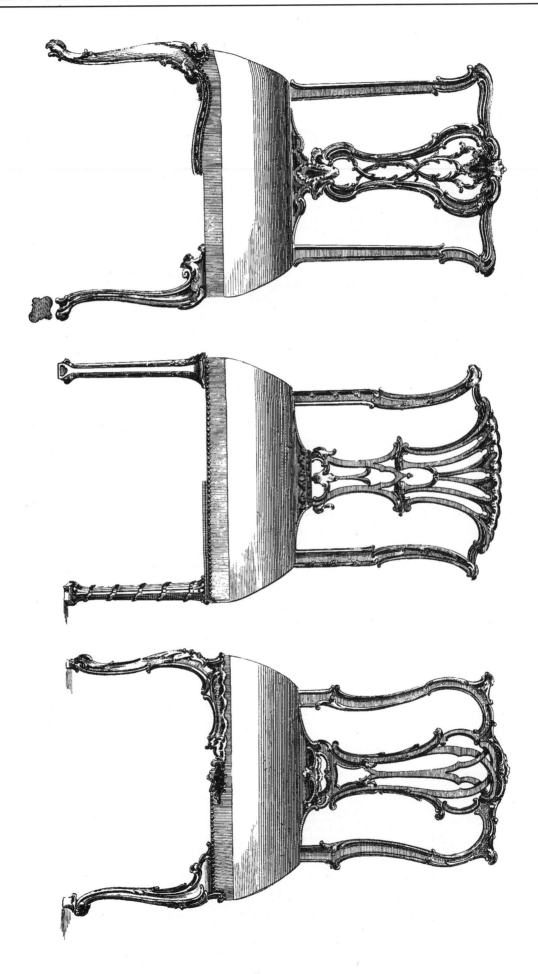

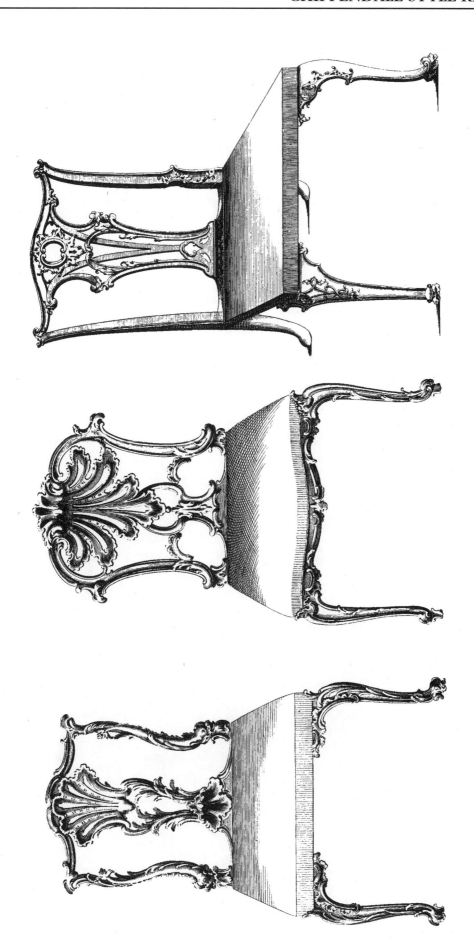

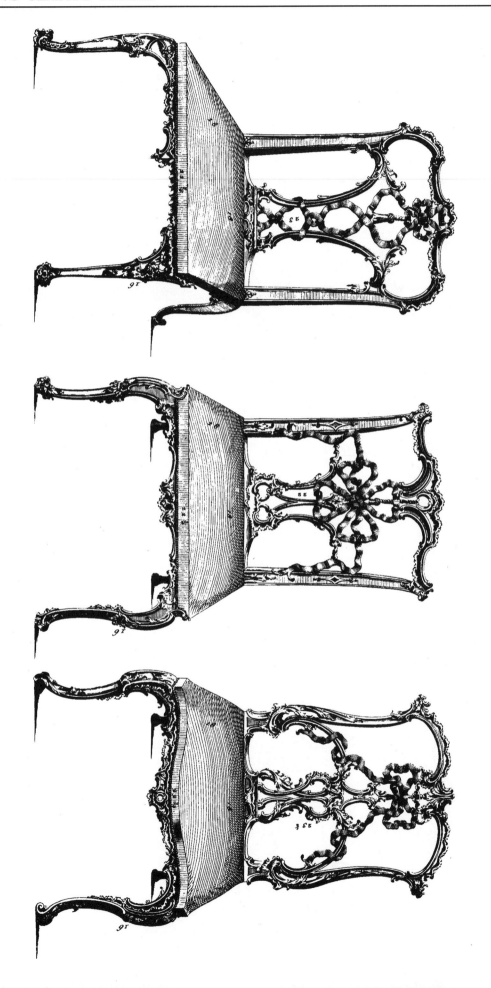

CHAPTER THREE

On Making Furniture Reproductions

On the subject of my "philosophy" about making reproductions, let me first say that I am working on a commercial level. I am making a living from creating reproductions; this is not a hobby for me, nor is it something done to make some extra money in addition to the earnings of a regular job. That fact, in itself, helps to more clearly define my philosophy regarding the making of reproductions.

In this book, you'll see me working not only with the hand tools, such as chisels, gouges and mallets, that were common during Chippendale's lifetime, but also with some of the newest power tools manufactured for today's woodworker. I use a bandsaw to cut the wood to shape, a router to create rabbits, an orbital sander to smooth the wood.... While it may seem contradictory to make reproductions with the help of new technology, I find this combination of older, authentic tools and modern electrically powered equipment allows me to create accurate reproductions in a timely manner.

I believe more credence is given to my use of power tools by a study of Thomas Chippendale himself and other master carvers of the 18th century. These craftsmen were also creating furniture as a means of financial support, and as soon as new technology was introduced, they took advantage of it. I firmly believe that Chippendale and his peers would be using our modern power tools if they were creating their furniture pieces today.

Another justification for my use of power tools comes from the differences in how a craftsman's shop was organized in the 18th century when compared with a shop today. In the 18th century, the apprenticeship system was in place. Anyone who wanted to become a master craftsman in any field had to work as an apprentice to a master craftsman for up to seven years. These apprentices, often as young as seven years old, would work for and learn the mysteries and secrets of the trade from a master craftsman in the field. After a successful apprenticeship, the apprentices would advance to become journeymen with increased responsibilities in the shop. Only after years of honing their skills could the journeymen apply to the members of a guild to become master craftsmen.

Shops were also very specialized during the 18th century. One craftsman did the carving, and other did turnings, a third worked on gilding, a fourth upholstered finished pieces of furniture, and so on. It was not unusual for a furniture maker to send the legs of a chair to be turned by a master turner and then returned to the furniture maker for assembly. Nor was it unusual for a third party to become involved when the chair was ready for upholstery.

Under this system of apprenticeship and specialization, a master craftsman would have had a handful of apprentices and journeymen working with him in his shop, as well as a host of other master craftsmen to aid him in finishing a piece of furniture. I, on the other hand, work alone. I have no apprentices or journeymen to help me in my shop. I also do all the work, such as the turning and the carving, myself (though I do send some pieces out for upholstering). In essence, my power tools become my apprentices and allow me to be a jack-of-all-trades.

I also use the same philosophy when it comes to staining my reproductions. While there are recipes available to duplicate the stains the masters of the 18th century created from natural sources, I prefer to make my own blend from commercial stains. I combine several different shades of brown until I get a pleasing tone for the piece on which I'm working. This gives a uniqueness to my pieces in that the coloring of no two pieces is identical.

I do, however, want to stress that where carving is concerned I rely solely on hand tools. In my experience, the modeling is the key to a successful reproduction, and using hand tools is the only way to achieve the exact look of the modeling on the original pieces.

Another quandary I've come across while making reproductions is how to exercise my own creativity when I'm trying to duplicate another's work. I rarely make an exact duplicate of a piece of furniture unless I'm required to do so by a client. More often, I find myself combining elements from the time period.

For example, the model for the chair I'm carving in the demonstration section of this book cannot be found. It resembles several chairs, but no other chair is its exact duplicate. That's because I changed the carving motifs on the legs and adapted the knee return carvings from various chairs. As a result, you won't find the original anywhere, but the piece is still immediately recognizable as 18th-century style furniture.

This type of "combination" work was outlined by Thomas Chippendale in his book *The Gentleman & Cabinet-Maker's Director*. He encouraged carvers to mix and match elements based on the client's needs and his ability to pay for the finished piece. A furniture maker could leave out certain carved elements or substitute simpler elements on a chair for a client whose budget was tight. For this reason, it is difficult to identify specific Chippendale-style furniture by comparing it to the patterns in the *Director*.

In my work, combining elements is more a result of my working style than the financial needs of my clients. I frequently work from photographs of the original pieces. Deciding what elements to use is often based on which photographs are the clearest.

Of course, one needs to be careful when combining elements. There is often a tendency to alter the elements, even if just slightly. And there is a world of difference between altering elements and creating different combinations of the original elements. I strive to combine elements, not alter them. To me, understanding the elements and being able to reconnect them shows more respect and creativity than altering.

I focus on carving reproductions of 18th-century American furniture because I find its style highly recognizable. Put a selection of furniture from the Irish, the French, and the English in a room with American pieces, and it's easy to tell the American pieces apart—without even opening a drawer or looking on the undersides of the pieces.

That uniqueness is due in part to the clientele of the 18th-century furniture-makers. They were sophisticated people with plenty of disposable income, making their fortunes from booming merchant and real estate industries. And in those days, to impress your peers, you had to spend money to buy things to show just how much money you had. It was not unusual for a family to refurnish an entire house for a special event such as a wedding. Their demands upon the furniture maker helped him to make furniture to the best of his ability.

Architecture also influenced the furniture of the 18th century. Modeling on pieces of furniture created by the masters often matched the architecture of the buildings. This is especially evident in furniture carved in 18th-century Philadelphia where architectural elements from mouldings, doors and windows become design elements on chairs, chests and tables.

I find that creating "new" furniture does not appeal to me. If you study 18th-century American furniture, you'll find that it is a veritable renaissance of design. The artists' ability for line and proportion is incredible. I've found no other time period where these are achieved with greater skill. In my 25 years of experience making furniture, I've found that duplicating that work to the best of my ability is far more challenging than creating something "new."

—Ron Clarkson

CHAPTER FOUR

Chair Anatomy and Measured Drawings

BILL OF MATERIALS

	Length	Width	Thickness	Quantity
Crest Rail	20$\frac{1}{2}$	3$\frac{1}{4}$	1$\frac{1}{2}$	1
Back Splat	17$\frac{3}{4}$	9$\frac{3}{4}$	1$\frac{1}{8}$	1
Rear Legs	36	5$\frac{1}{2}$	1$\frac{3}{4}$	2
Shoe	13$\frac{1}{4}$	1$\frac{5}{8}$	1$\frac{5}{8}$	1
Back Rail	15$\frac{1}{8}$	3$\frac{3}{4}$	$\frac{7}{8}$	1
Side Rails	16$\frac{3}{4}$	3$\frac{3}{4}$	$\frac{7}{8}$	2
Front Rail	19$\frac{3}{4}$	3$\frac{3}{4}$	$\frac{7}{8}$	1
Front Legs	17	3	3	2
Knee Blocks	11	3	3	4

*makes 2   Note: This cutting list is applicable to both Chair #1 and #2

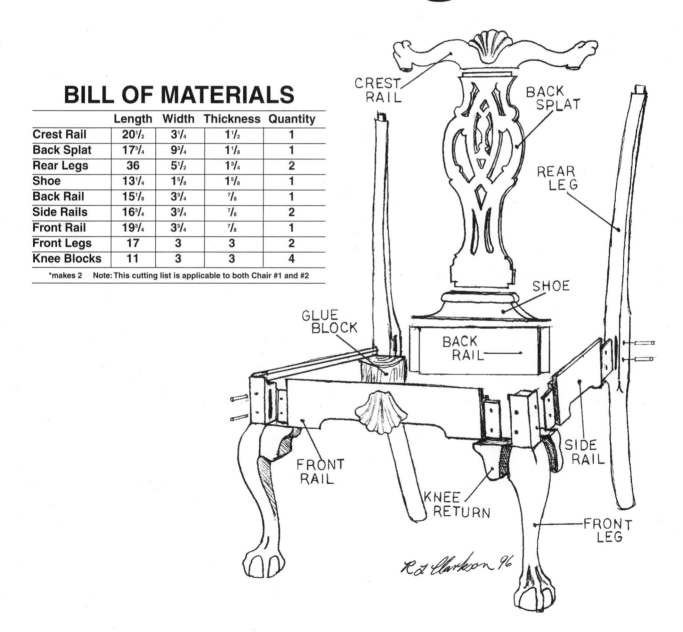

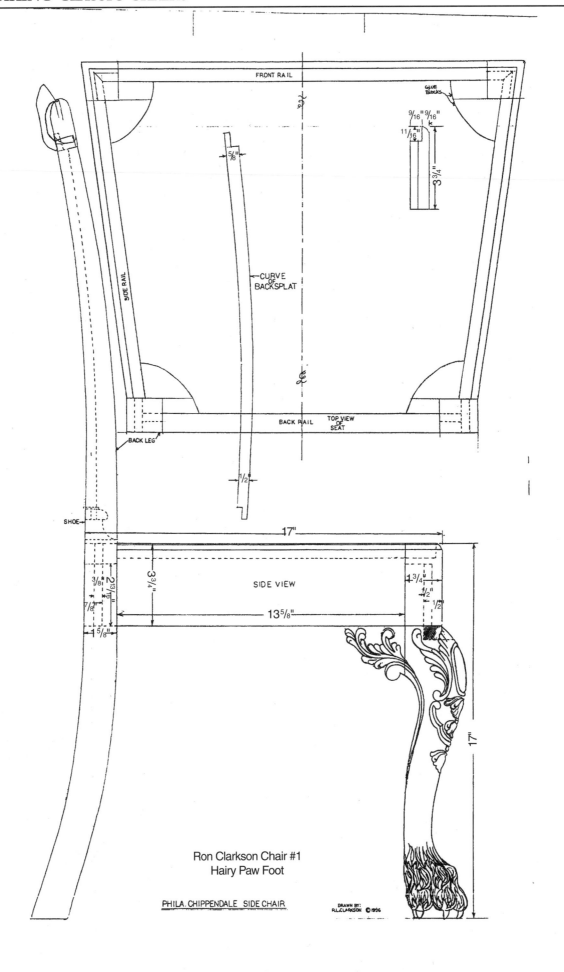

FRONT RAIL

GLUE BLOCKS

9/16" 9/16"

11/16"

3 3/4"

5/8"

SIDE RAIL

CURVE OF BACKSPLAT

BACK RAIL

TOP VIEW OF SEAT

BACK LEG

SHOE

1/2"

17"

3/8"

2 13/16"

3 3/4"

SIDE VIEW

1 3/4"

1/2"

1/2"

7/8"

13 5/8"

1 5/8"

17"

Ron Clarkson Chair #1
Hairy Paw Foot

PHILA. CHIPPENDALE SIDE CHAIR

DRAWN BY:
R.L.CLARKSON © 1996

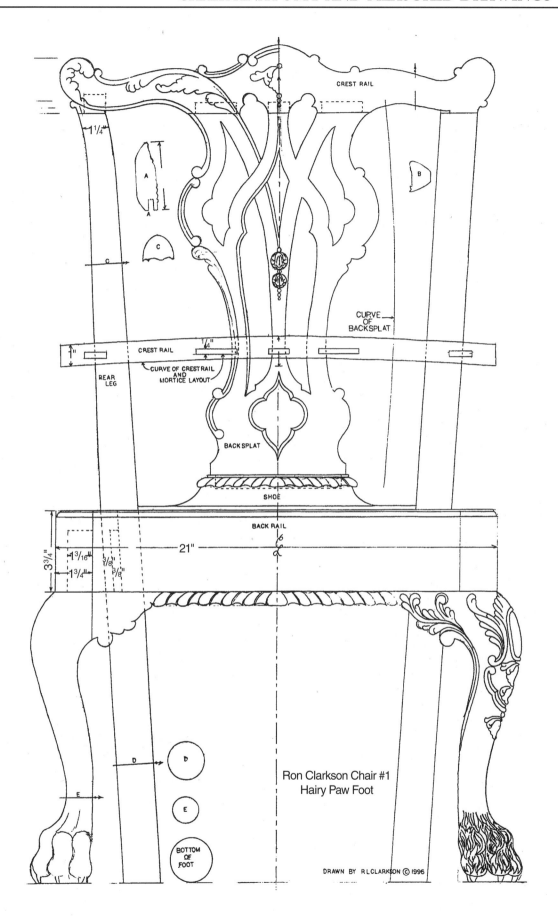

CREST RAIL

1¼

A

A

C

B

CURVE
OF
BACKSPLAT

CREST RAIL

1"

¼"

CURVE OF CREST RAIL
AND
MORTICE LAYOUT

REAR
LEG

BACK SPLAT

SHOE

BACK RAIL

3¾"

1³/₁₆"

3/8"

1¾"

3/8"

21"

D

D

E

E

BOTTOM
OF
FOOT

Ron Clarkson Chair #1
Hairy Paw Foot

DRAWN BY R.L.CLARKSON © 1996

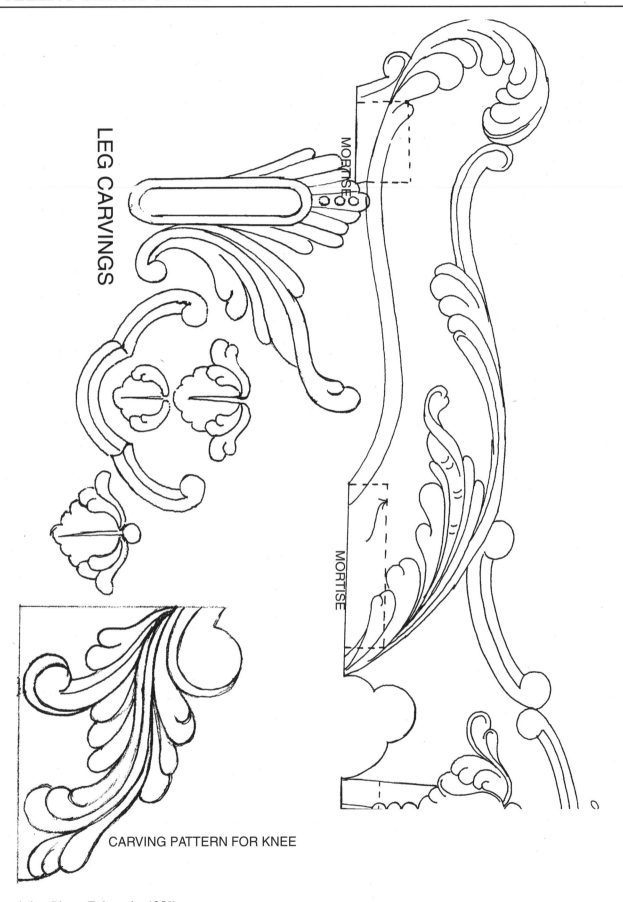

LEG CARVINGS

MORTISE

MORTISE

CARVING PATTERN FOR KNEE

Reduced size. Please Enlarge by 125%

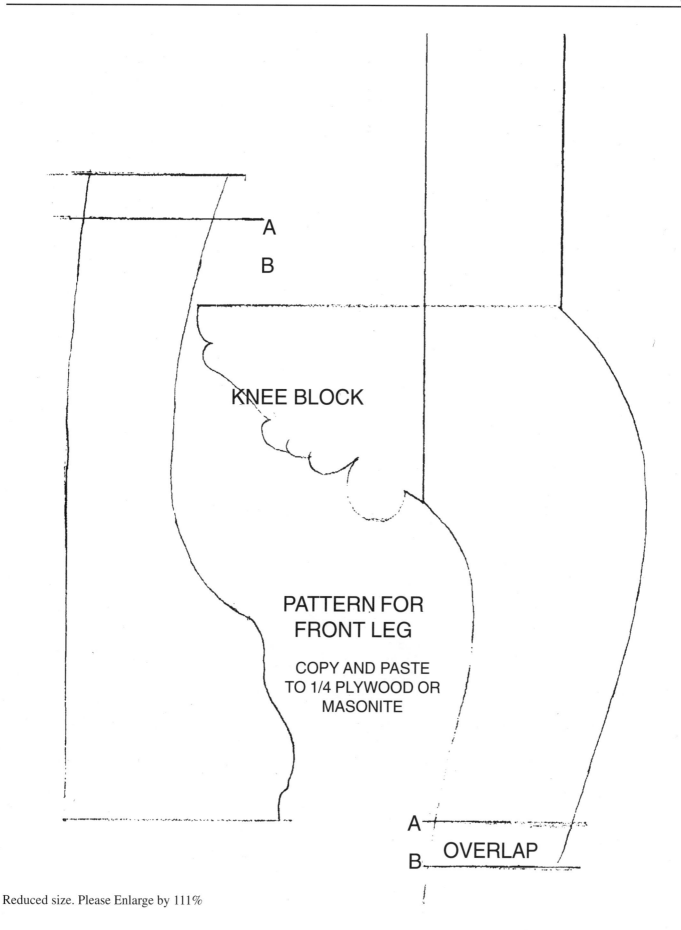

A

B

KNEE BLOCK

PATTERN FOR
FRONT LEG

COPY AND PASTE
TO 1/4 PLYWOOD OR
MASONITE

A

B OVERLAP

Reduced size. Please Enlarge by 111%

ADD TENON

R.L. Clarkson © 96

Reduced size. Please Enlarge by 111%

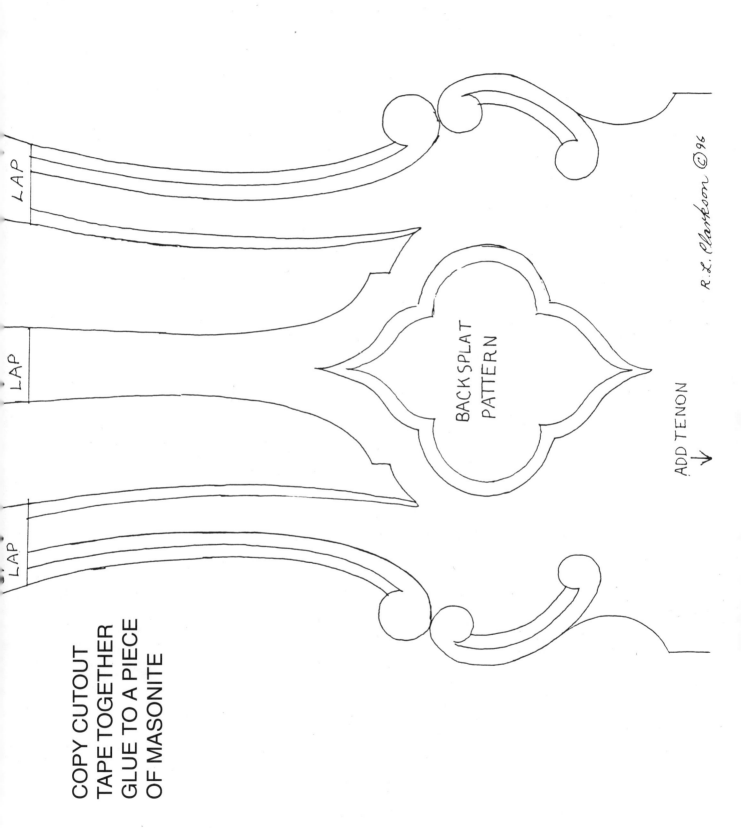

BACK SPLAT PATTERN

LAP

LAP

LAP

ADD TENON

R.L. Clarkson ©96

COPY CUTOUT
TAPE TOGETHER
GLUE TO A PIECE
OF MASONITE

Reduced size. Please Enlarge by 111%

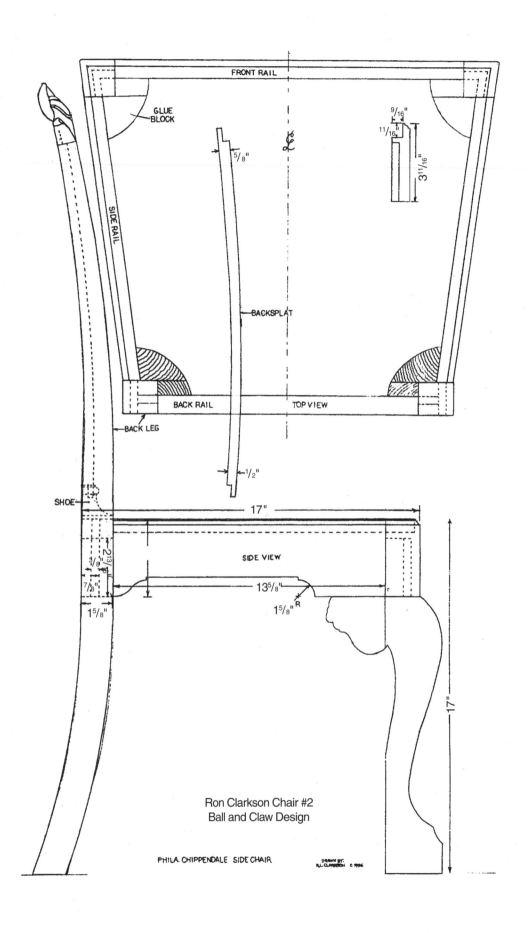

FRONT RAIL

GLUE BLOCK

SIDE RAIL

5/8"

9/16"
11/16"
3 11/16"

BACKSPLAT

BACK RAIL   TOP VIEW

BACK LEG

1/2"

SHOE

17"

SIDE VIEW

2 13/16"
3/8"
7/8"
1 5/8"

13 5/8"

1 5/8" R

17"

Ron Clarkson Chair #2
Ball and Claw Design

PHILA. CHIPPENDALE SIDE CHAIR

DRAWN BY:
R.L. CLARKSON C 1996

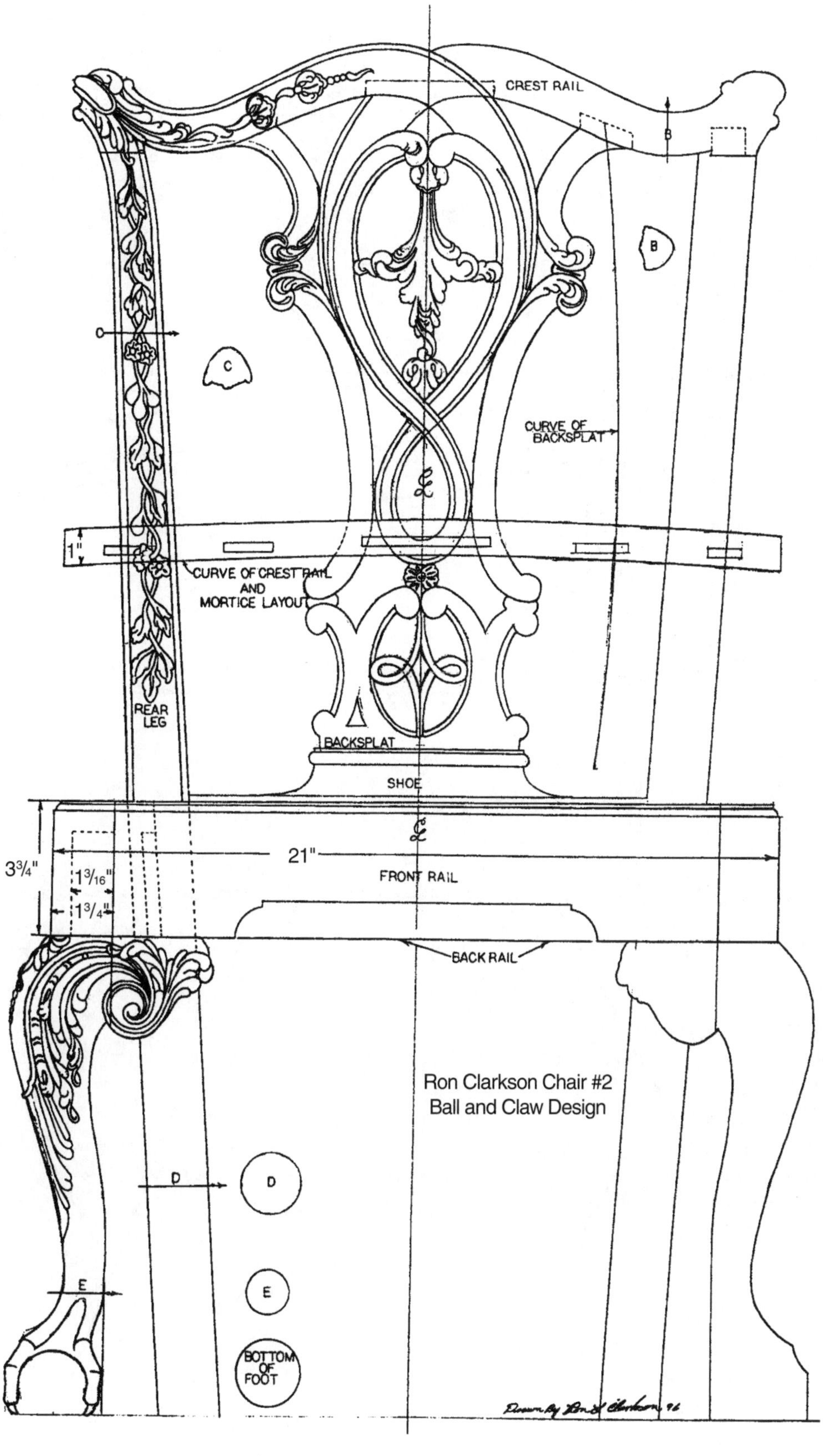

CREST RAIL

B

B

C

C

CURVE OF
BACKSPLAT

1"

CURVE OF CREST RAIL
AND
MORTICE LAYOUT

REAR
LEG

BACKSPLAT

SHOE

3¾"

1³/₁₆"

1³/₄"

21"

FRONT RAIL

BACK RAIL

Ron Clarkson Chair #2
Ball and Claw Design

D

D

E

E

BOTTOM
OF
FOOT

Drawn By Ron J Clarkson 96

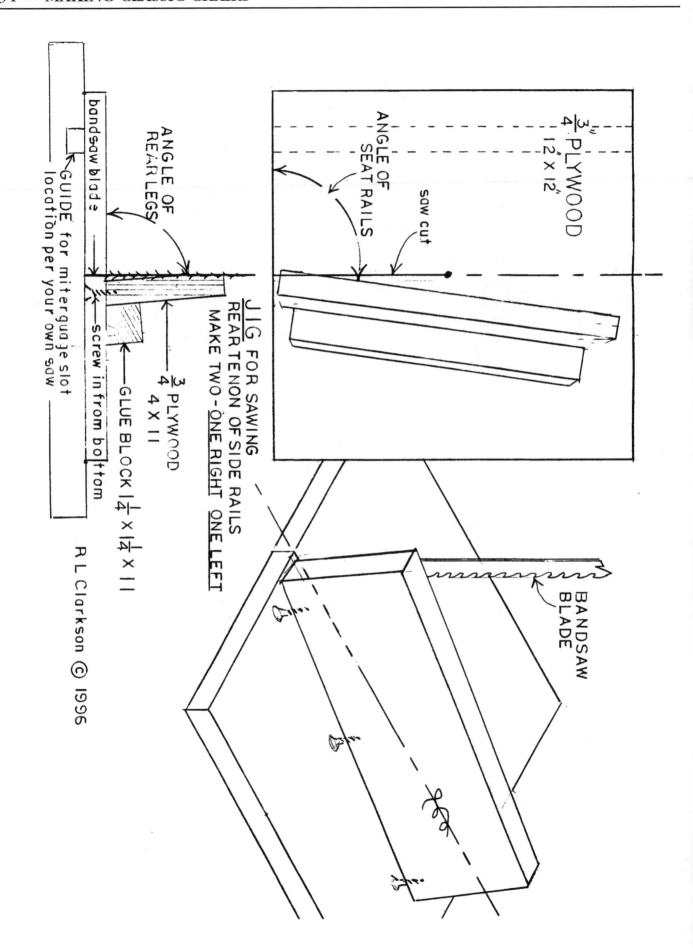

$\frac{3}{4}$" PLYWOOD 12" x 12"

ANGLE OF SEAT RAILS

saw cut

ANGLE OF REAR LEGS

bandsaw blade

GUIDE for miter gauge slot
location per your own saw

screw in from bottom

$\frac{3}{4}$ PLYWOOD 4 X 11

GLUE BLOCK 1$\frac{1}{4}$ × 1$\frac{1}{4}$ × 11

JIG FOR SAWING
REAR TENON OF SIDE RAILS
MAKE TWO - ONE RIGHT ONE LEFT

R L Clarkson © 1996

BANDSAW BLADE

CHAPTER FIVE

Tools and Safety

Many artists new to making furniture reproduction may find themselves tempted to purchase an overwhelming number of tools before starting their first project. The temptation is hard to resist due to the number of different tools available to today's woodworkers, but well worth the effort. I've found that it's best to start with a basic set of carving tools and accumulate more tools as you become more proficient in the art of woodworking.

And believe me, you will find plenty of tools to accumulate!

My shop is literally filled with tools. In the past 25 years I've had the opportunity to purchase a wide variety of the best tools from dealers, antique stores and even yard sales.

This list of basic carving tools will get you started on any woodworking project, not just furniture reproduction. (You'll find additional tools pictured in this chapter as well.)

> #2-5mm straight gouge
> #5-12mm straight gouge
> #5-16mm straight gouge
> #7-10mm straight gouge
> #8-7mm straight gouge
> #8-10mm straight gouge
> #8-16mm straight gouge
> #9-5mm straight gouge
> #9-10mm straight gouge
> #11-1mm veiner

#11-3 veiner
#15-6mm v-parting tool
#25-10mm back bent gouge

I've always believed in buying the best tools available and recommend that to any woodworker. Of course, buying the best doesn't always mean you have to buy the most expensive. Shop around. Ask other woodworkers. Read books and magazines. You'll find that buying the best is a good investment.

If you have a smaller shop, look into the new combination tools now available. You'll sacrifice production time to switch the tool from one phase to another, but if space is limited, this is a workable sacrifice.

One sacrifice you do not want to make is safety. And if you let common sense dictate your actions, you will be making the first step in the right direction. The following common sense safety steps should keep you moving in the right direction. While these pointers may seem obvious, they are often overlooked during the carving process.

Instructions. Always read the manufacturer's instructions in their entirety. Be sure to understand what you read.

Understand the tool's limits and never use a tool for anything other than its intended purpose. Pushing a tool beyond its limits, whether it's running a power tool on too little power or using a hand tool in an awkward position, is dangerous. Period.

Never use a power tool when you're tired or when you're hungry. Your mind tends to wander away from your work leaving you at a severe disadvantage.

Never use a power tool when you're in a hurry. Using and controlling power tools is a methodical, determined operation. If you don't have time to do it right, don't do it.

Make sure the tool is operating properly. If the power source for your saw is not large enough and the saw is bogging down, fix the power source. Blade guides need to be working. Blades need to be set into the saw properly. And so on.

Be comfortable. If the room in which you're working is too cold, the cold could lessen the sense of touch in your fingers; too hot and the tool could slip out of sweaty hands.

Have your eyes checked. If you're not hitting the lines, chances are you'll be hitting your fingers.

Plan time in your project for sharpening hand tools. A dull tool is your enemy. A dull edge requires more work to cut the wood and could cause you to lose control of the tool.

And don't forget about adequate ventilation, dust collection systems, goggles, and external fireproof storage areas for flammable products and rags.

Keep safety, and common sense, utmost in your mind while you're carving and you'll be carving for a long time to come.

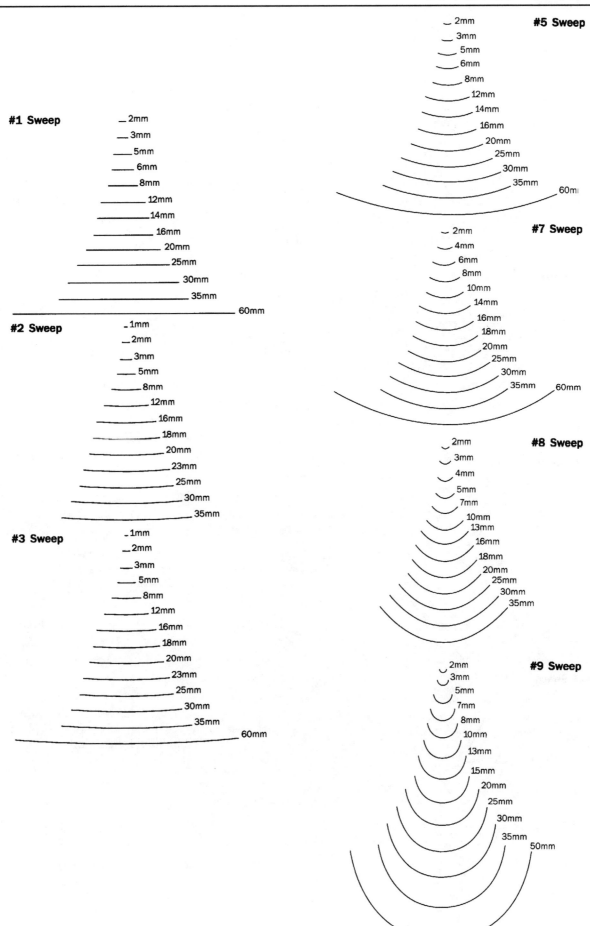

#1 Sweep

2mm
3mm
5mm
6mm
8mm
12mm
14mm
16mm
20mm
25mm
30mm
35mm
60mm

#2 Sweep

1mm
2mm
3mm
5mm
8mm
12mm
16mm
18mm
20mm
23mm
25mm
30mm
35mm

#3 Sweep

1mm
2mm
3mm
5mm
8mm
12mm
16mm
18mm
20mm
23mm
25mm
30mm
35mm
60mm

#5 Sweep

2mm
3mm
5mm
6mm
8mm
12mm
14mm
16mm
20mm
25mm
30mm
35mm
60mm

#7 Sweep

2mm
4mm
6mm
8mm
10mm
14mm
16mm
18mm
20mm
25mm
30mm
35mm
60mm

#8 Sweep

2mm
3mm
4mm
5mm
7mm
10mm
13mm
16mm
18mm
20mm
25mm
30mm
35mm

#9 Sweep

2mm
3mm
5mm
7mm
8mm
10mm
13mm
15mm
20mm
25mm
30mm
35mm
50mm

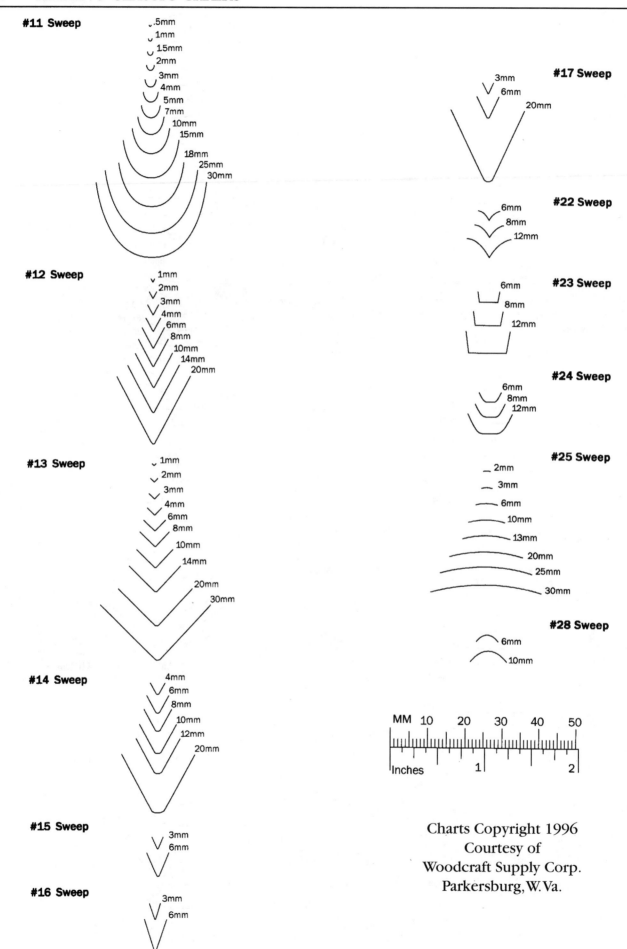

#11 Sweep

.5mm
1mm
1.5mm
2mm
3mm
4mm
5mm
7mm
10mm
15mm
18mm
25mm
30mm

#12 Sweep

1mm
2mm
3mm
4mm
6mm
8mm
10mm
14mm
20mm

#13 Sweep

1mm
2mm
3mm
4mm
6mm
8mm
10mm
14mm
20mm
30mm

#14 Sweep

4mm
6mm
8mm
10mm
12mm
20mm

#15 Sweep

3mm
6mm

#16 Sweep

3mm
6mm

#17 Sweep

3mm
6mm
20mm

#22 Sweep

6mm
8mm
12mm

#23 Sweep

6mm
8mm
12mm

#24 Sweep

6mm
8mm
12mm

#25 Sweep

2mm
3mm
6mm
10mm
13mm
20mm
25mm
30mm

#28 Sweep

6mm
10mm

MM 10 20 30 40 50

Inches 1 2

Charts Copyright 1996
Courtesy of
Woodcraft Supply Corp.
Parkersburg, W. Va.

CHAPTER 6

The Crest Rail and the Backsplat

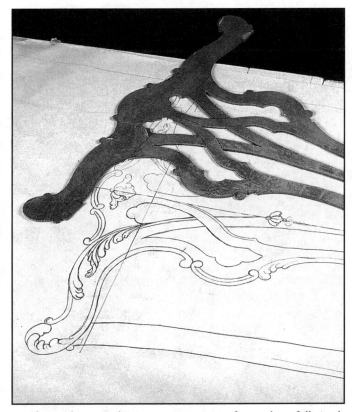

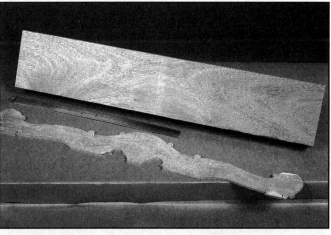

2 – Make a full-sized pattern of the crest rail based on your drawing and the measurements of the actual chair. Masonite or ¼" plywood is a good material for patterns that will be used repeatedly.

1 – If you plan to make your own patterns, first make a full-sized drawing of the back of the chair to help you make an accurate pattern.

3 – Using the pattern you made of the crest rail or the pattern included with this book, position it on a piece of mahogany stock, 3 x 21 x 1⅛". Trace around the outline of the pattern with a pencil or pen.

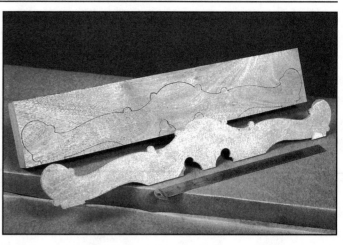

4 – The resulting drawing fits well within the boundaries of the mahogany piece and is aligned with the grain of the wood.

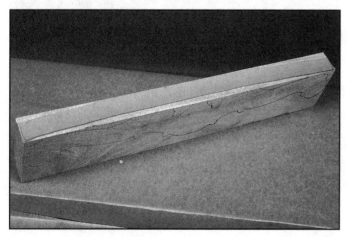

5 – Trace the pattern of the curve of the crest rail on the bottom or on the top of the piece of the mahogany.

6 – Starting with the curved part of the crest rail, bandsaw the back of the curve first. (If you are unfamiliar with any of the power tools I'm using throughout this demonstration, be sure to read and understand all safety instructions provided by the manufacturer before proceeding.)

7 – With a marking gauge set at the proper thickness, scribe a line parallel to the curve across the top of the crest rail.

8 – Use a bandsaw to cut along the marks you've just drawn for the front of the curve.

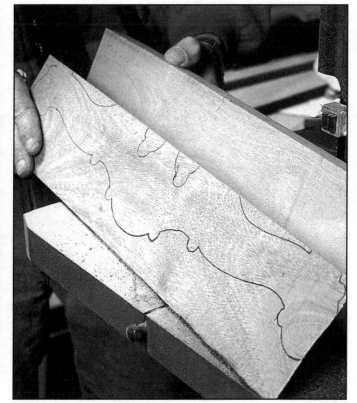

9 – Save the piece that you removed from the front of the crest rail with the bandsaw. You may need it later to help hold the crest rail in the mortising machine.

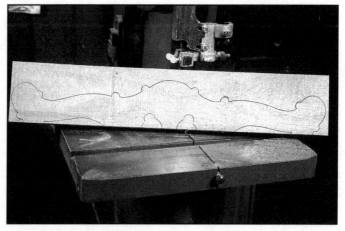

10 – Using the pattern for the front of the crest rail, redraw the pattern on the front of the crest rail piece.

11 – Cut out the pattern on the bandsaw.

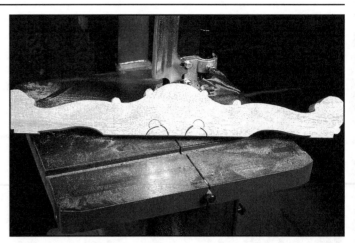

12 – Note that the small curves on the bottom of the crest rail are too tight to cut with a bandsaw.

13 – The best way to remove the wood from this area is to use a ³/₄" forsner bit.

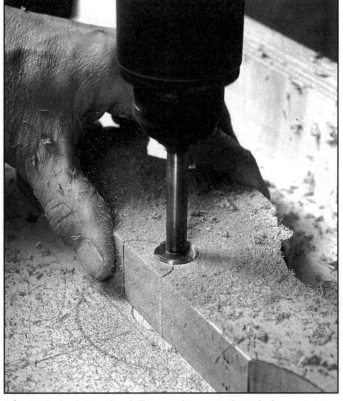

14 – With the bit in the drill press, bore out these holes.

15 – It will take several passes to completely remove the wood in this area.

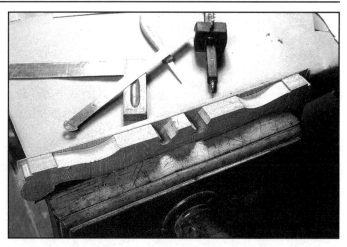

16 – Clamp the crest rail and the piece you cut away from the front curve into a vise, bottom side up. You'll need a ruler, a square, marking knife and a marking gauge.

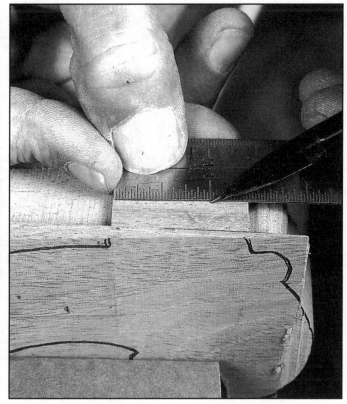

17 – Starting with the back leg mortises, go over 1" from the inside cut and make a mark.

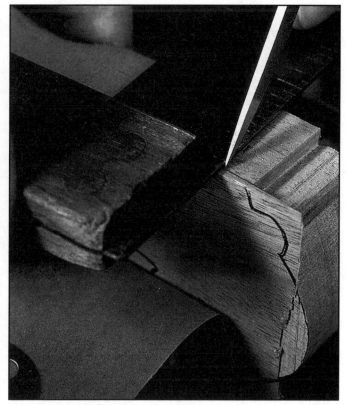

18 – With a square, scribe the outside line across the bottom of crest rail.

19 – This line that you just made will be the outside line for the mortise.

20 – From the front of the crest rail, measure in ¼" from the front of the crest rail. (The front of the crest rail is concave.)

21 – Then make a mark ½" in from the front of the crest rail. These two marks will establish a ¼" mortise for the back legs.

22 – Set your marking gauge and scribe the mortises down the length of the crest rail.

23 — Notice that the mortises are scribed parallel to the front edge of the piece that you removed from the crest rail and not parallel to the curved front edge of the crest rail itself.

24 — Measure ¼" and ½" to mark the shoulders of the mortises for the backsplat. These measurements should be taken from the cut line.

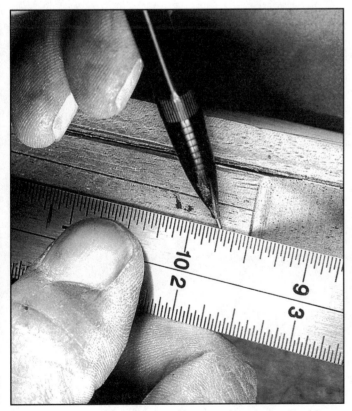

25 — Measure in ¼" from the profile cut and mark the shoulders for the outer members of the back splat on the crest rail.

26 — The resulting markings for the mortises should be placed on the crest rail like those in this photo.

27 – A stationary mortising machine is used to remove wood from the mortise. First line up the bit with the mortise lay out.

28 – Use the mortising machine to chop out the mortise.

29 – The mortise will look like this when you are finished.

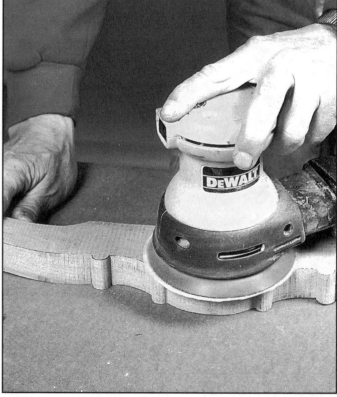

30 – Now is a good time to do some preliminary sanding with a random orbital sander. Sanding now will make it easier to transfer the patterns later.

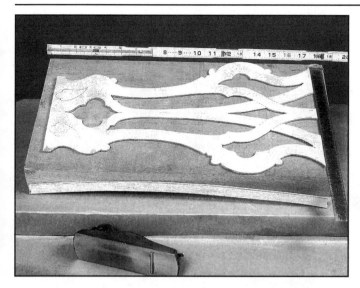

31 – Move on to the backsplat. Start with a piece of mahogany 18½" x 9¾" x 1½".

32 – Mark the center of the backsplat by measuring the width and dividing it by two.

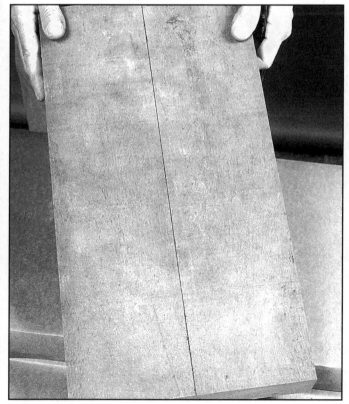

33 – Using your mark as a guide, draw a line with a pencil down the center of the backsplat. This divides the backsplat in half vertically.

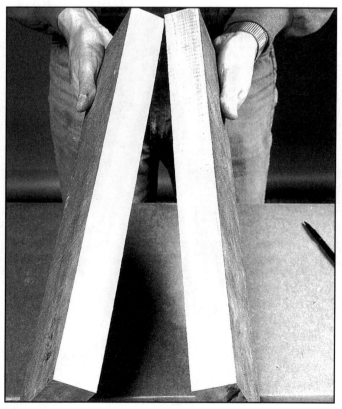

34 – With the bandsaw, saw the backsplat in half.

35 – Place the pattern on the edges exposed by the bandsaw cut, and mark the curve of the backsplat on each piece.

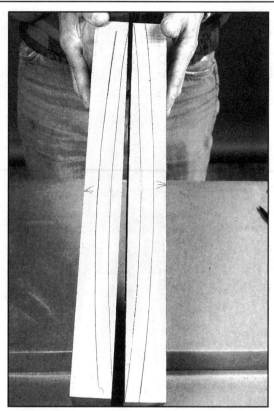

36 – The curves should be marked as those shown on this piece.

37 – Take each piece to the bandsaw and carefully cut along the pattern lines.

38 – The resulting bandsaw cuts will leave you with two pieces of wood similar to these.

Philadelphia Side Chair, 1755-1795.
(Courtesy of Museum of Fine Arts, Boston) *Gift of Mr. and Mrs. Maxim Karolik Collection.*
See Leigh Keno's chapter "Chippendale Furniture and the Chippendale Style" for a
discussion of this chair and other antique examples found on the following pages.

Chippendale Mahogany Scroll-foot Side Chair, circa 1765
(Courtesy Leigh Keno)
Carving attributed to the shop of Nicholas Bernard and Martin Jugiez, Philadelphia

Chippendale Mahogany Side Chair, circa 1765
(Courtesy Leigh Keno)
Carving attributed to the shop of Nicholas Bernard and Martin Jugiez, Philadelphia

Chair Design #1 - Ball and Claw by Ron Clarkson

Features a fully carved back starting with a crestrail combining cabochon, acanthus and bellflower carving, flowing into a strapwork pierced backsplat with a central carved element. Both rear legs are carved, as are the acanthus design front legs which terminate in ball and claw feet.

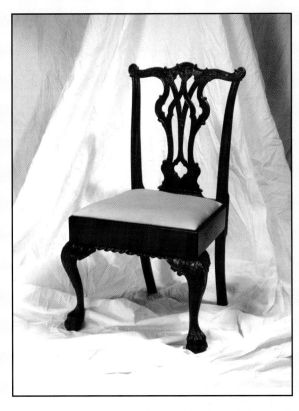

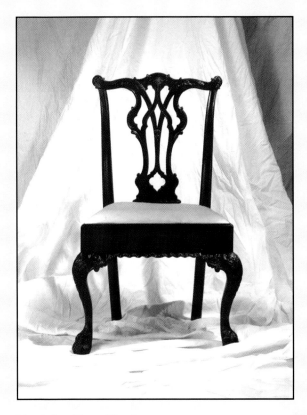

Chair Design #2 - Hairy Paw Foot by Ron Clarkson

Features an acanthus and C scroll carved crest rail flowing into a pierced carved Gothic splat, terminating with a gadrooned carved shoe. A plain front skirt and gadrooned apron are flanked by cabochon and acanthus carved legs which end in articulated hairy paw feet.

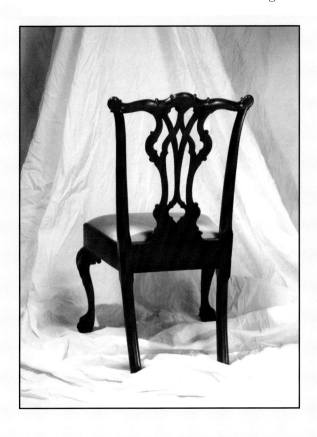

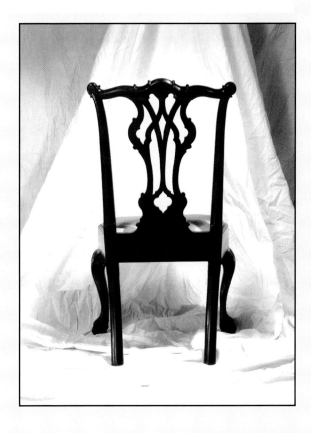

Knee Detail - Hairy Paw Chair
Showing cabochon with acanthus leaves flowing away, ending in C scrolls.

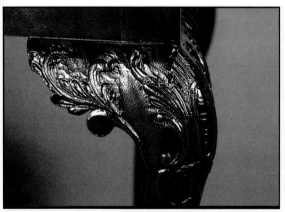

Knee Detail - Hairy Paw Chair
(Left) Side view, left front leg. *(Right)* Front view, left front leg.

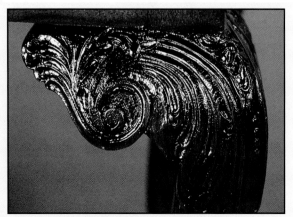

Knee of Ball and Claw Chair
Showing acanthus design flowing
out of the center C scroll

Ball and Claw Chair
This design reflects a typical
Philadelphia-style foot

Details - Ball and Claw Chair

(Left) Detail of strapwork backsplat with carved center pendant. *(Right)* Vine leaves detail.

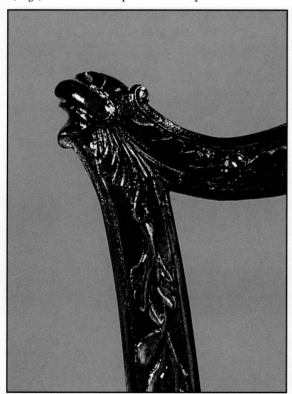 

Details - Ball and Claw Chair

(Left) Detail of the ear showing juncture of cabochon and vine leaf designs.
(Right) Detail of bellflower carving on crestrail and backsplat acanthus leaf design.

Hairy Paw Chair - Detail Photographs

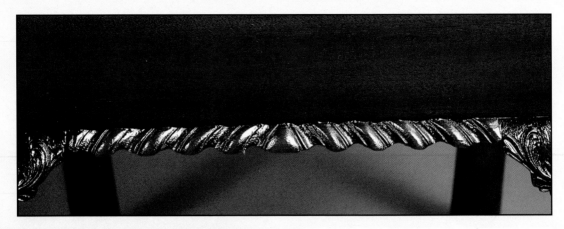

(Above) Showing gadroon carved
element of front seat rail.
(Left) Gothic backsplat with
bellflowers and C scroll.

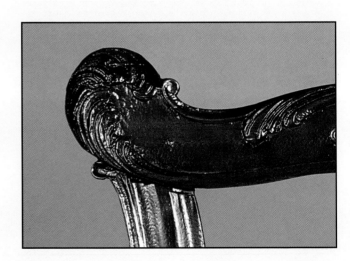

Note how the acanthus leaf design flows up from the
backsplat onto the crestrail.

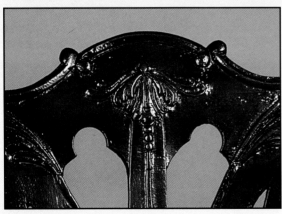

(Left) Bellflower and bead design carved in the center of the crestrail.

(Right) Ear of crestrail. Note how the acanthus leaf pattern
appears to spill over from the back of the crestrail onto the front.

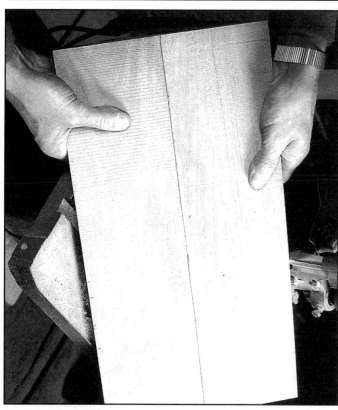

39 – After both halves have been cut out, check to see how they line up according to the grain of the wood.

40 – Apply glue liberally to both pieces and clamp them together tightly.

41 – Note that if you have access to a larger bandsaw, you can cut out the backsplat from a solid piece.

42 – With a low angle block plane and a sharp blade, begin to true up both faces of the backsplat by making a thin cut. This process begins with the front of the backsplat clamped firmly in a vise. Begin planing across the grain.

43 – Work your way across the entire surface of the backsplat, truing up the face as you progress.

44 – The result of your work should be an evenly planed surface that eliminates any bandsaw marks.

45 – Now, prepare to smooth the surface of the backsplat with a standard cabinet scraper blade.

46 – Before I begin, I prepare the scraper blade by filing the edge of the blade perfectly flat with a fine-cut file.

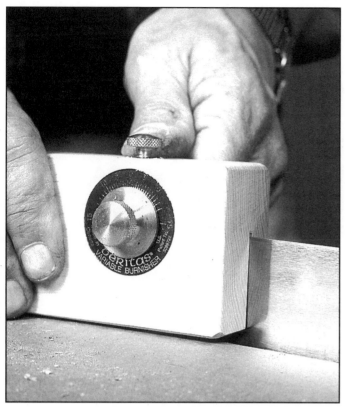

47 – Using a burnisher, in this case a Veritas variable angle burnisher, I put an approximate 15-degree hook angle on the blade.

48 – When the blade is angled to my satisfaction, I place the blade in the scraper holder, which helps to create the necessary bow in the blade.

49 – Begin scraping the surface of the backsplat, following the grain direction, to eliminate any marks left from hand-planing across the grain.

50 – After the scraping has been completed, cut the board to its final dimensions. From the rough bottom edge, come down approximately ½" and make a mark.

51 – Next come down the face of the backsplat approximately 17½" and make another mark.

52 – With a square, mark a horizontal line across the top.

53 – Square up the ends of the backsplat with a table saw.

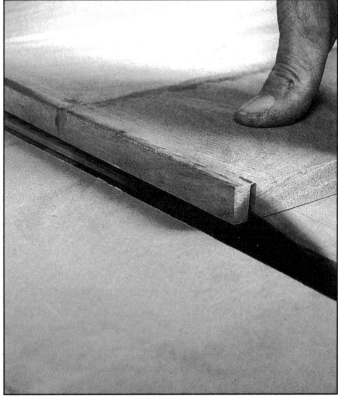

54 – Then trim off the end.

55 – Repeat the process for the bottom by scribing a horizontal line along the other mark and trimming off the end.

56 – After the backsplat has been trimmed to its proper dimensions, begin laying out the tenon at cither end. Mark up from the bottom ½" first.

57 – With a marking gauge set to ½", scribe a line all the way across the board to achieve an accurate parallel line.

58 – The resulting line should look like the one in this photo.

59 – Next we will mark in from the front of the backsplat ¼". This will be the thickness of the tenon.

60 – Use a marking gauge set to ¼" to scribe a line across the backsplat.

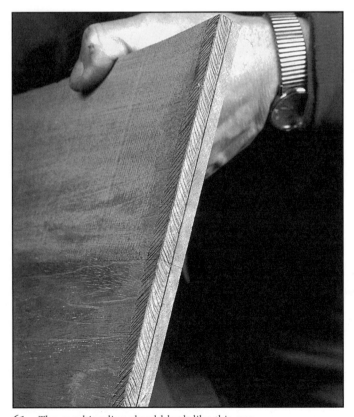

61 – The resulting line should look like this one.

62 – Use a router and router table to rabbet out the shoulder of the bottom tenon of the backsplat. First, set a ½" rabbitting bit to the proper depth.

63 – Then begin rabbitting. (Again, be sure to read and understand all of the manufacturer's directions before using any equipment that is new to you.)

64 – Make sure that the wood is pressed firmly against the top of the table.

65 – Also make sure the end of the board is pressed firmly against the fence.

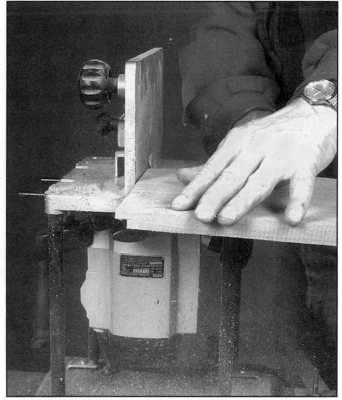

66 – Continue rabbitting until the cut is made.

67 – The resulting rabbet cut should look like this.

68 – With the pattern of the backsplat laid on the front and lined up with the bottom shoulder, mark the tenons for the crest rail.

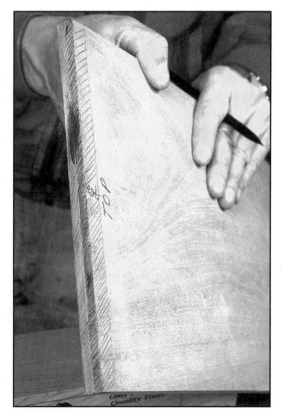

69 – Use a router and router table to rabbet out the top tenon as well.

70 – Repeat the rabbetting process using the same set up as we used for the bottom tenon.

71 – The resulting cuts will look like this.

72 – Now with the backsplat pattern laid on top of the board, begin tracing the outline of the backsplat.

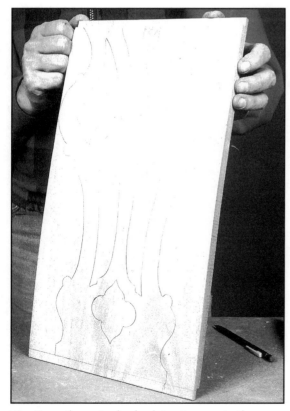

73 – Trace the entire backsplat pattern on to the wood. Your lines should be dark and very visible.

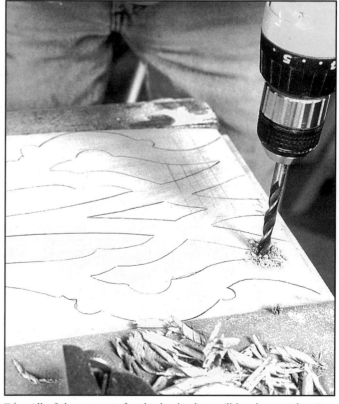

74 – All of the cut-outs for the backsplats will be done with a jig saw, so starter holes have to be drilled for the inside cuts.

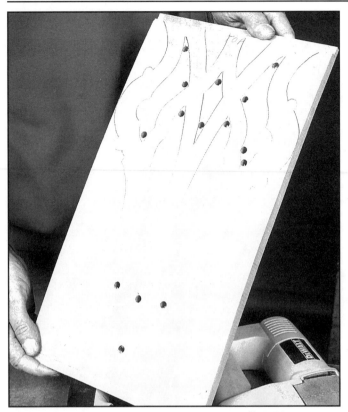

75 – Drill several holes in each cut-out with a ¼" drill bit.

76 – With the board firmly clamped, begin sawing using a 1⅞ x ¼" 12-tooth-per-inch blade.

77 – Follow along the pencil lines to cut out the inside areas of the patterns. These cuts will be smoothed out later.

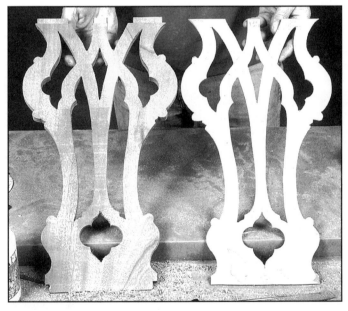

78 – Compare the pattern to the backsplat and make any necessary adjustments before moving on.

79 – Lining up the backsplat with the crest rail, you can now mark the shoulders of the tenons.

80 – With a small beading saw, remove the wood on each side of the tenon.

81 – The result of the cuts made with a beading saw will look like this.

82 – At this point, the tenons and mortises should line up perfectly.

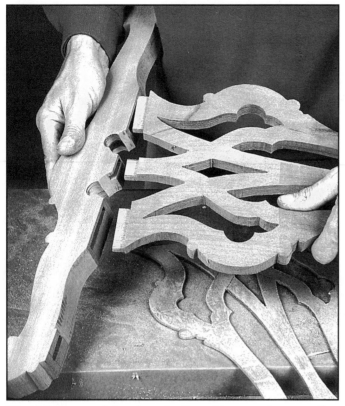

83 – Now is a good time for a dry fit, making sure the crest rail and backsplat are in line.

84 – With the crest rail and backsplat fitted together, clamp them down to the top of the bench. Align the curvature of the crest rail and that of the backsplat with a sander.

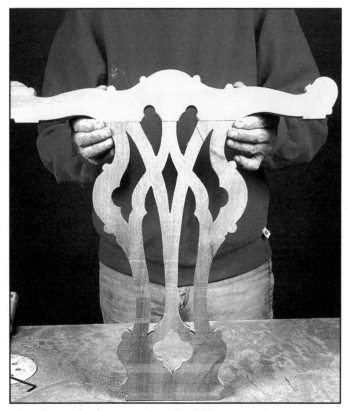

85 – The result of your sanding should be a smooth transition between both pieces.

CHAPTER 7

Detailing the Backsplat

Floral Elements

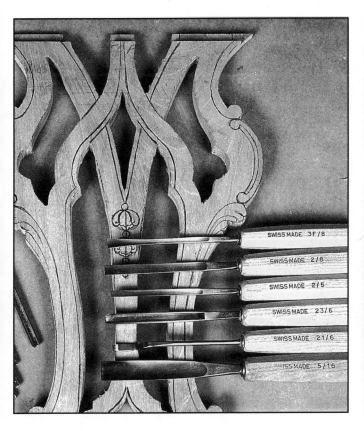

1 – Using the drawings included with the patterns, layout the backsplat so that we can begin to carve it. The photograph shows which tools are to be used.

2 – Starting at the areas where the backsplat appears to overlap, begin setting in with a ¼" straight chisel, approximately ³⁄₁₆" in depth.

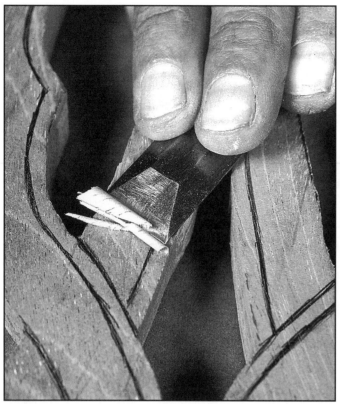

3 – Using a flat chisel, pare wood away up to the line you just set in. Don't worry about cutting away the line. It can be redrawn later.

4 – The results of the cuts should look like this.

5 – With a macaroni carving tool, set the raised portion or bead as indicated on the pattern.

6 – This photo shows the resulting bead.

7 – Once again, with a flat chisel, level this area.

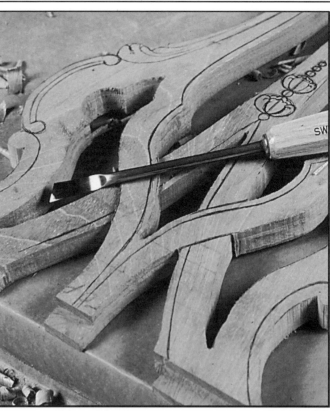

8 – There are times when the angles of the pattern will not allow a flat chisel to reach the corners. This is when a bent skewed chisel works the best.

9 – The bent skewed chisel will allow you to work angled areas where the bars of the backsplat seem to overlap.

10 – Begin setting in the flowered portion of the backsplat. These cuts should be 3/16"-1/4" deep. Choose your gouges to correspond with the curves of the flowers.

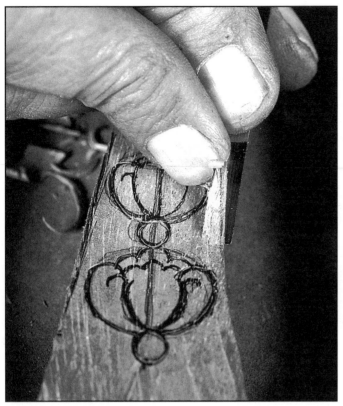

11 – After the setting in process has been completed, relieve the wood surrounding the flowers.

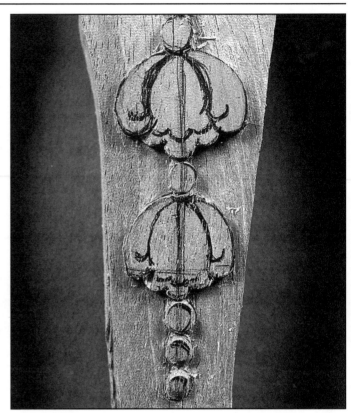

12 – First complete one side, then the other.

13 – Now begin detailing the flowers with a variety of tools.

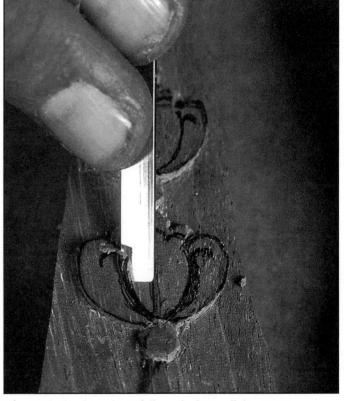

14 – Work slowly and carefully and, above all, be patient.

15 – At the bottom of each flower are small ruffles. These will need to be set in also.

16 – Begin relieving the wood inside these cuts until the flowers look like this.

17 – Be sure to note which way the grain runs. Sometimes you may have to reverse your cutting to get the best results.

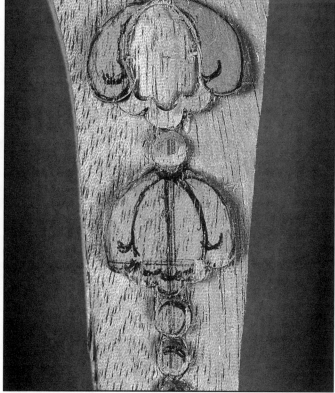

18 – Continue to relieve the flowers.

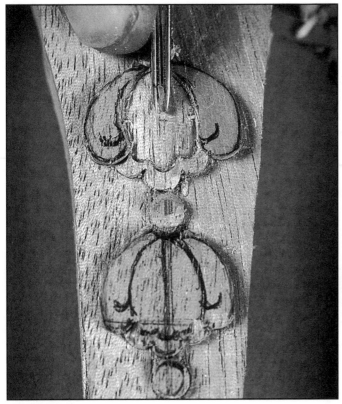

19 – With a #2 veiner, begin adding detail to the flowers.

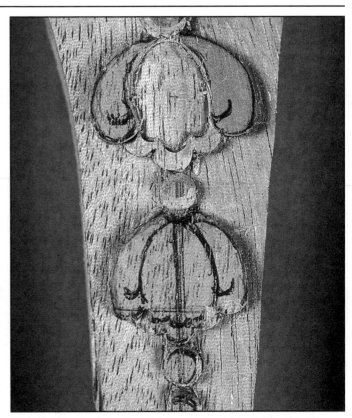

20 – The result of the first detail cuts should look like this.

21 – Next set in the outer petals.

22 – With the next larger chisel, make a release cut.

23 – Then begin rounding the outer portions of the petal.

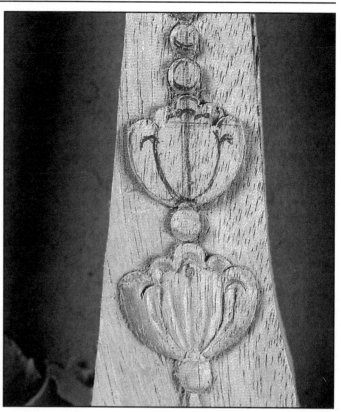

24 – The outer portions of the petal should look like this.

25 – The detail carving is now completed.

26 – Cut the small cove in the quatrefoil at the bottom of the backsplat with an 8/4 gouge.

27 – Do both sides to get this result.

CHAPTER 8

Honing Your Tools

1 – Now would be a good time to discuss the honing of your chisels. With various shaped ceramic stones, a piece of leather, some honing compound and rouge, you will be able to regain a sharp edge on your dulled tools.

2 – Starting with the ceramic stones, touch the edge lightly.

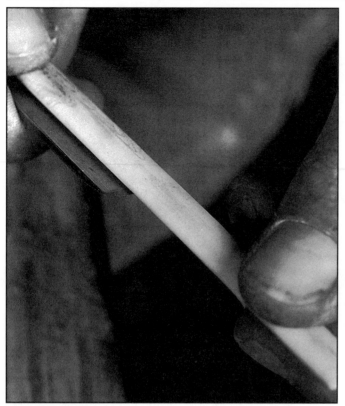

3 – With the appropriately curved stone, repeat the process on the inside, making sure to keep the stone flat.

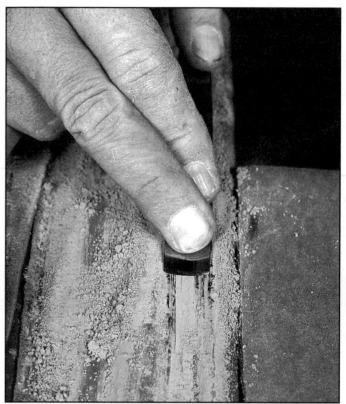

4 – With honing compound sprinkled on the length of the leather, begin to strop the chisel, making sure to keep the angle constant.

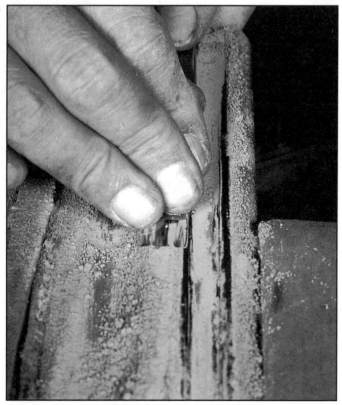

5 – Repeat for the other side of the chisel, but be sure the chisel is flat. You do not want an inside bevel.

CHAPTER 9

Detailing the Crest Rail

Floral Elements and C-Scrolls

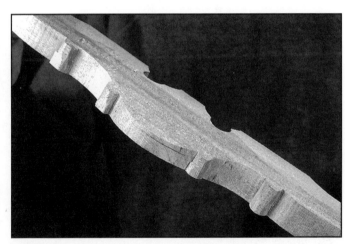

2 – The resulting contour should match that of the crest rail shown in this photograph.

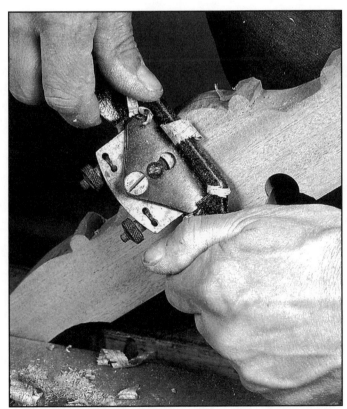

1 – Now, turn your attention to the crest rail. With a spoke shave, begin contouring the front of the crest rail at the top center.

3 – Next contour the entire back of the crest rail using a flat chisel.

4 – With the front and back of the crest rail contoured, the piece will look like this.

5 – Copy the drawing in the pattern section of this book. Then cut it out and paste it on the front of the crest rail with rubber cement.

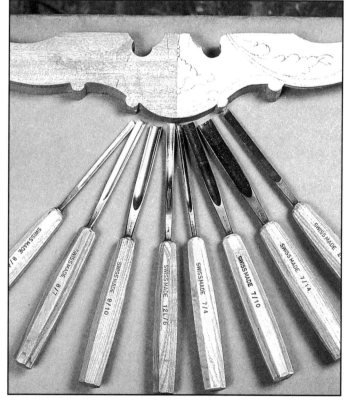

6 – Begin working on the carving on the front of the crest rail. The setting-in process will require a number of sweeps, mainly 7's and 8's.

7 – Begin setting-in around the outline of the drawing. Repeat this procedure on the other side of the drawing.

8 – A detail shot of the setting in process shows how these first cuts should be made.

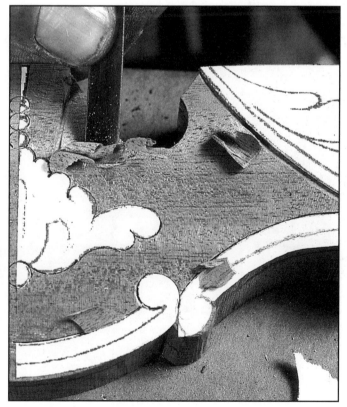

9 – Once you have set in around your pattern, you can remove the background paper.

10 – Then begin relieving the wood up to the set-in areas.

11 – The resulting cuts should relieve the drawing like this.

12 – After you have completely set in around your drawings, you will need to transfer your modeling lines onto the wood. This can be done by placing a piece of carbon paper between the pattern and the crest rail and tracing over the lines with a pencil.

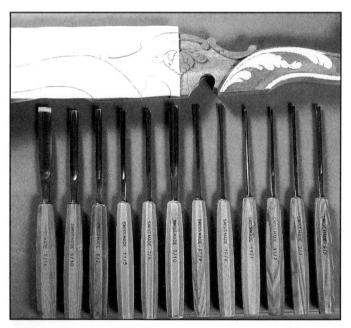

13 – Once again you will need an assortment of profiles and sweeps to do the modeling.

14 – Begin setting in on your transfer lines.

15 – Now start to profile your carving.

16 – Continue profiling your carving.

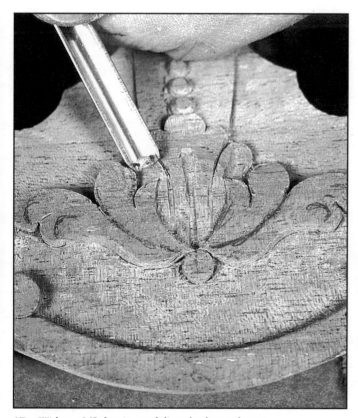

17 – With a #8/5, begin modeling the lower leaves.

18 – Continue modeling the lower leaves.

19 — With a #2 veiner, you can add your detail.

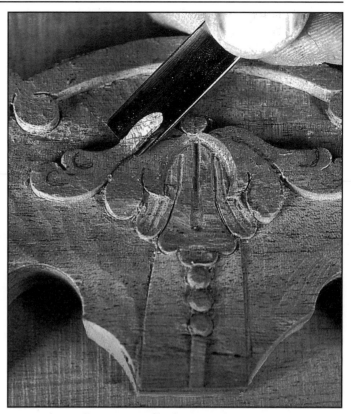

20 — With a #8/7 start to profile the upper leaves.

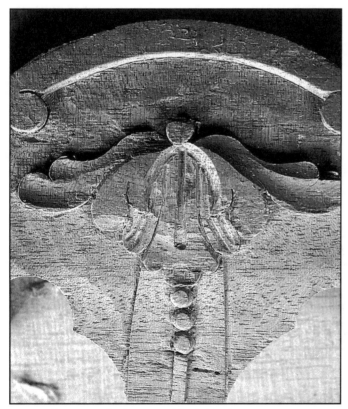

21 — At this point, the leaves will look like this.

22 — This photo shows the finished, unsanded carving.

23 – With an appropriately curved gouge, round over the top portion of the center C–scroll.

24 – The top portion will appear rounded.

25 – Next with a #8/7, make the inner cut of the C–scroll.

26 – In this case, you'll need to come from both sides to the center, following the grain.

27 – The resulting scroll will look like this. Note that you can now complete the other C-scroll and finish the carvings in the center of the crest rail using the same procedures.

CHAPTER 10

Making the Shoe

1 – Because the rest of the carving on the crest rail requires all of the back to be assembled, you'll now have to make the shoe in which the backsplat will rest. You'll need a block of wood, 1½" x 1½" x 13¼", and the pattern from the book.

2 – Start by finding the center of the block of wood.

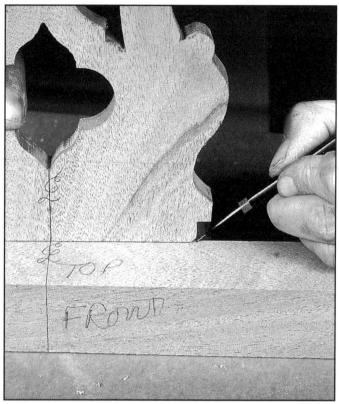

3 – With the backsplat placed over the center, mark out for the width of the mortise.

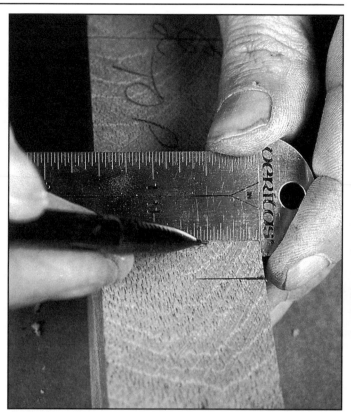

4 – Now from the back of the shoe, come in ½" and make a mark.

5 – Then make another mark ¼" from the back of the shoe.

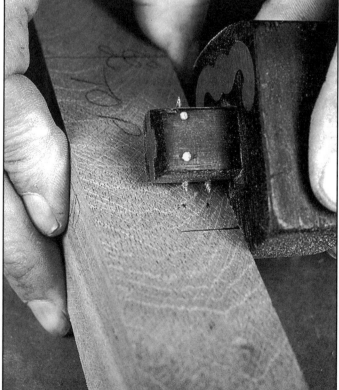

6 – With a marking gauge, scribe this line across the width of the mortise.

7 – The resulting marks will indicate the mortise. Note that there are a number of ways in which a mortise can be cut. The simplest way is by a stationary mortising machine. I'll show you several methods, including a mortising chisel.

8 – Starting at the end of the mortise, begin by chopping out the mortise.

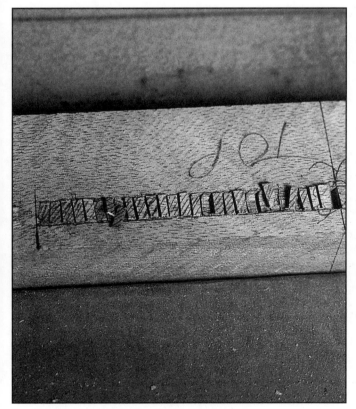

9 – The wood will look like this as you progress.

10 – Once you have chopped out the mortise, relieve the chips of wood until the entire mortise has been cleared of chips.

11 – Another method you can employ is the use of a drill press and a ¼" drill bit.

12 – Simply drill consecutive holes along the length of the mortise until the area is completely filled with drilled holes..

13 – Now with a flat chisel, pare down the sides and take out all the waste between the drillings.

14 – The resulting mortise will look like this.

16 – Begin to lay out the profile of the shoe using the pattern in the book.

15 – Before progressing any further, make sure the backsplat fits tightly into the shoe.

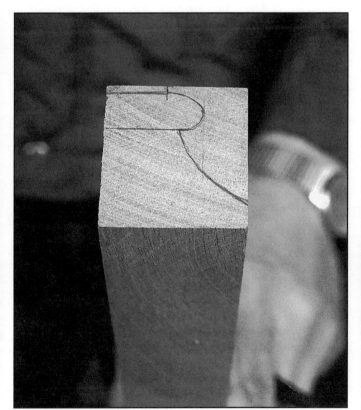

17 – Also transfer the profile to the end of the block.

18 – Once all the lines have been transferred, begin cutting them away using a table saw. The table saw setting will correspond to the pattern line.

19 – Starting at the top of the shoe, make your first cut, which will be the top profile above the gadrooning.

20 – Next we will make a cut with the blade set at ⅝" high.

21 – Moving the fence over, make the cut for the bottom gadrooning.

22 – The resulting cut will look like this.

23 – Now remove the small piece to give you the front face of the gadrooning.

24 – Continue to make the cut.

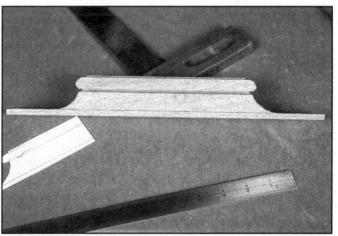

26 – With a bandsaw, cut out the profile of the shoe.

25 – The resulting cut will look like this.

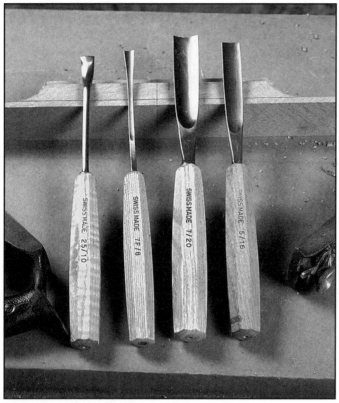

27 – Using a shouldered rabbet plane, a #25/10 back bent round over gouge, a #7/8 fish tail, a #7/20, a #4/16 and a low angled block plane, begin contouring the front of the shoe.

28 – Starting with a #5/16, begin removing material from the front of the shoe.

29 – Continue removing wood from the front of the shoe until the front is completed.

30 – With a #7/20, begin to define the profile of the shoe.

31 – The result will look like this.

32 – With the #7/8 fish tail, clean up the area underneath the gadrooning area.

33 – With the rabbetting plane, begin rounding over the area to be gadrooned.

34 – It is easier to do the underneath part with a back bent gouge.

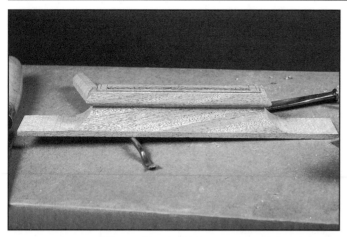

35 – Continue until the underside of the area is completed.

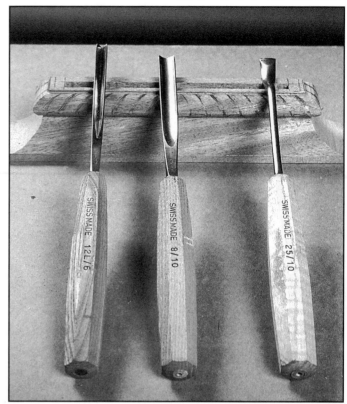

36 – Begin carving the gadrooning using a v-gouge, a #8/10 and a #25/10 back bent.

37 – After laying the lines according to the patterns in the book, begin carving with the v-gouge.

38 – Repeat the process by continuing around to the other side.

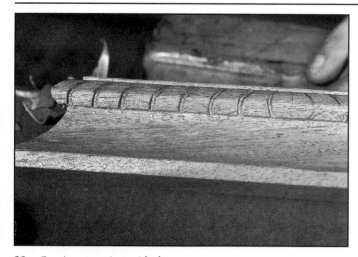

39 – Continue carving with the v-gouge.

40 – With a #8/10 gouge, carve the underside of all the concave segments.

41 – Continue carving the concave segments.

42 – With a flat bench chisel, begin rounding the convex elements into the v-gouge cuts.

43 – The result will look like this.

44 – Now with the gouge, begin doing the concave segments.

45 – Continue working with the gouge until all the concave segments are completed.

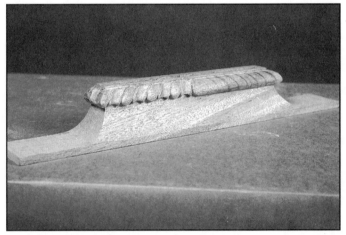

46 – The resulting cuts will look like this.

CHAPTER 11

Shaping the Legs

1 – Now turn your attention to the back legs. The legs are taken from 8 quarter stock with sufficient height and width to accommodate the pattern.

2 – After bandsawing your stock, locate and cut your mortises as shown in the plans.

3 – After the mortising is completed, shape the back legs. Various coarse and fine rasps and spoke shaves are required for this part of the project.

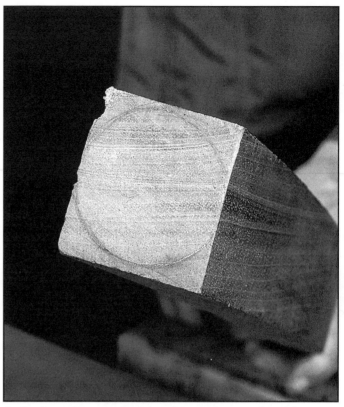

4 – Begin work on the back legs by marking a circle on the bottom of the leg.

5 – From the bottom of your mortise, mark down approximately 1". This will be your stopping point for the shaping.

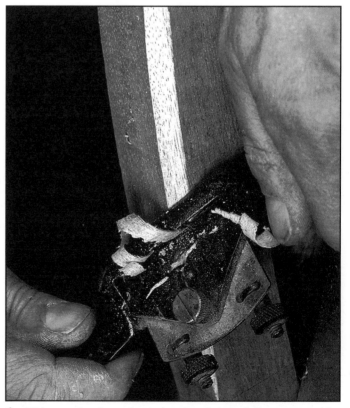

6 – With a spoke shave, begin by chamfering all four corners of the lower part of the leg.

7 – Once the four corners of the leg have been chamfered, move to the upper part of the bottom of the leg.

8 – At the top part of the leg ease the chamfer in, using a half round coarse rasp.

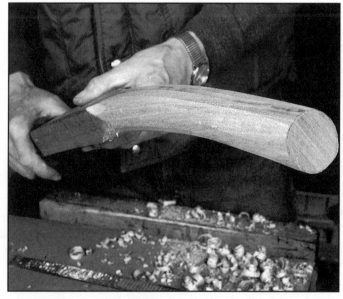

10 – Continue to work with the spoke shave until the leg is rounded.

9 – After the chamfering is completed on the top and bottom portions of the lower part of the leg, begin rounding over using the same spoke shave.

11 – With a half round spoke shave, finish truing up the bottom part of the leg.

12 – The bottom part of the leg should now be nicely rounded.

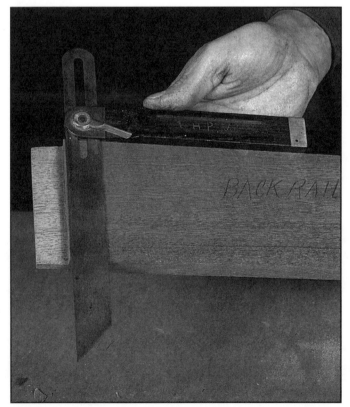

13 – Following the pattern in the book, you can now make the back rail. With a sliding bevel, mark the angle of the shoulders and cut out the tenons.

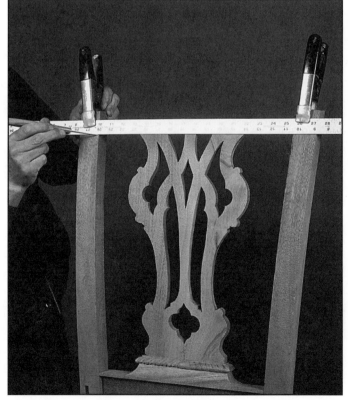

14 – With the back rail, shoe, backsplat and two back legs assembled dry, lay out the shoulders for the tenons of the two back legs. Clamp a straight edge to the two back legs where they align with the shoulder of the tennon of the backsplat and mark across with a knife.

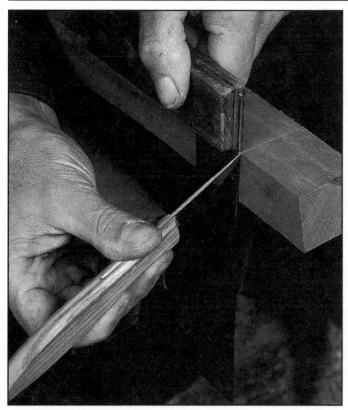

15 – Disassemble the chair and clamp the back leg into the vise. With a square placed on the front face of the back leg, mark the side shoulders.

16 – The resulting marks should look like this.

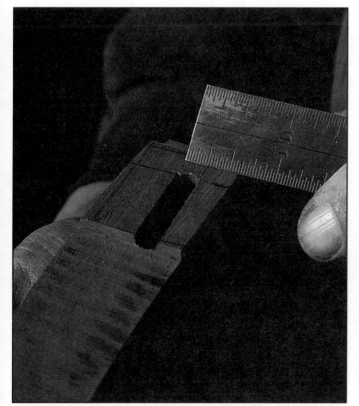

17 – Take measurements from the mortise in the crest rail and transfer them to the top of the back chair leg.

18 – A marking gauge works well for transferring the measurements to the top of the leg.

19 — The resulting marks will look like this.

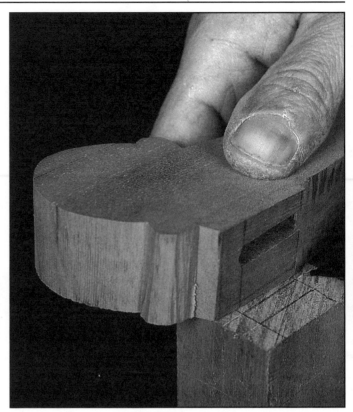

20 — With the crest rail positioned on the top of the back leg, mark the inside and outside shoulders.

21 — With a backsaw, begin sawing out the tenon.

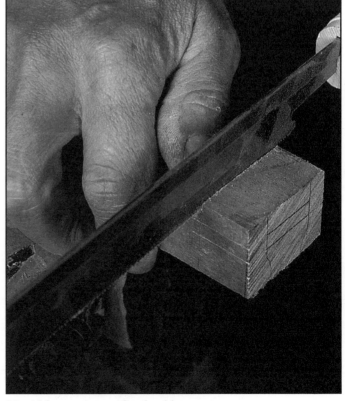

22 — Make sure to cut the shoulders square.

23 – The tenon has been cut out of the back leg.

24 – Using the pattern as a guide, mark the front profile of the back leg.

25 – With a bandsaw, cut the front profile and remove the waste.

26 – Shape the top part of the back leg as you did with the lower part of the leg.

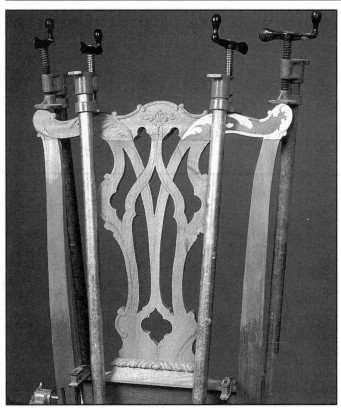

27 – Using cabinet makers glue, glue and clamp the back together. Allow the glue to dry according to the directions. Excess glue can be removed with a rasp once the glue has dried.

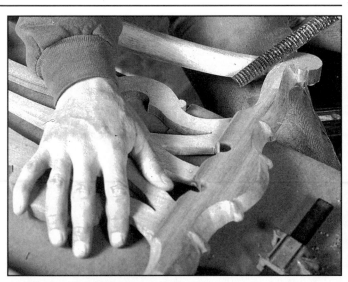

28 – Now you can shape all of the areas with rasps and files where the crest rail and back rail meet.

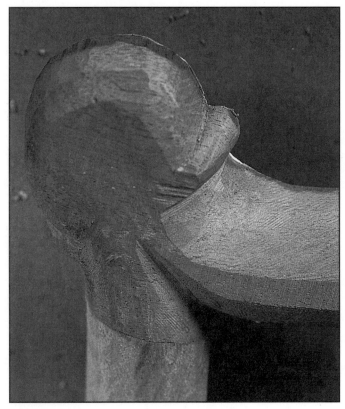

29 – The leg has been attached and nicely shaped.

30 – Finish up by rough shaping around the back part of the ear of the crest rail with rasps and chisels.

CHAPTER 12

Joining the Backsplat and Crest Rail

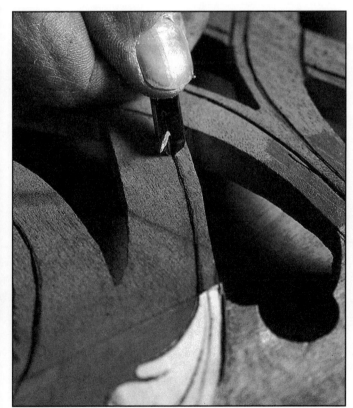

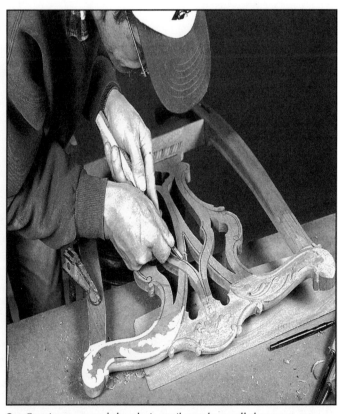

1 – Now we can join elements from the backsplat to the crest rail. With a v-gouge, set in the line you have drawn.

2 – Continue around the chair until you have all the areas set.

3 – With a flat bench chisel, remove the wood in the flat areas between the raised areas.

4 – With the appropriate gouges, begin setting in the leaf carvings of the crest rail with a #9/5 and a #9/6 gouge.

5 – The photo shows the process of setting in with assorted chisels.

6 – With the background removed, this is the result.

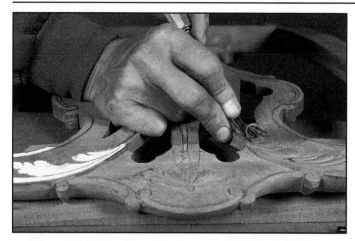

7 – The same process for modeling as used earlier will be used on these leaves.

8 – Continue modeling the leaves.

9 – With a small #1 veiner, add some detail to the leaves.

10 – As the grain changes, sometimes it is necessary to change the direction of your carving to match the grain.

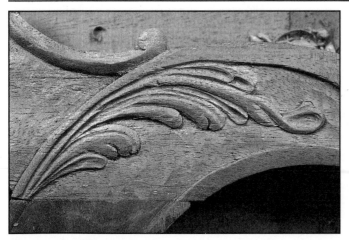

11 – Patience here will reward your efforts.

12 – Now turn your attention to the ear of the crest rail. As you can see, it has already been set in.

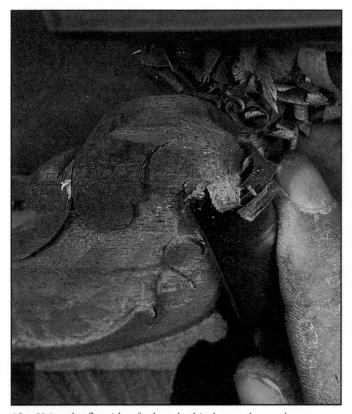

13 – Using the flat side of a bench chisel, round over the ear toward the back.

14 – With the ear rounded, you are ready to move on to modeling the front part of the back leg.

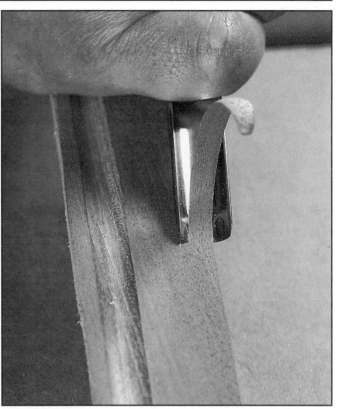

15 – Begin by taking a #8/10 gouge and make a gouge cut down the back leg. This will create a molding-like appearance on the back leg.

16 – With the same gouge, run a groove to the inside of the back leg.

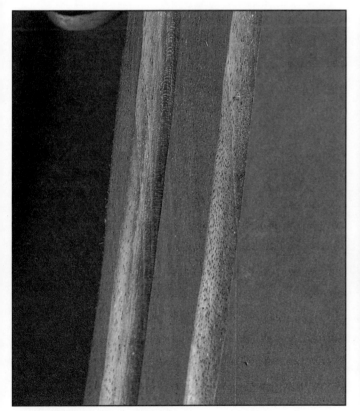

17 – Continue to make the groove in a smooth cut.

18 – There are at least two methods to round over the area between the two gouge cuts. You can use a #25/20 back bent in this area.

19 – Or you can use the flat part of a bench chisel.

20 – Continue this process all the way up into the crest rail.

21 – After completing the cuts for both of the concave grooves, continue rounding the middle part of the back leg.

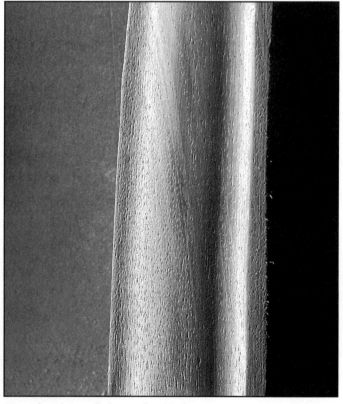

22 – After doing all the work with the gouges, you can sand out the marks left by the chisels.

23 – With a #9/5, cut a small groove on the outside of the back leg.

24 – This groove should run all the way up into the crest rail.

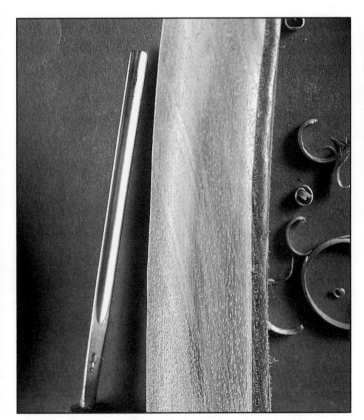

25 – The resulting groove is a little rough and needs to be smoothed.

26 – A piece of sandpaper rolled up will help smooth out this area.

27 – After you have finished cutting the molding of the back leg, finish the modeling of the back ear of the crest rail.

CHAPTER 13

Shaping and Detailing the Feet

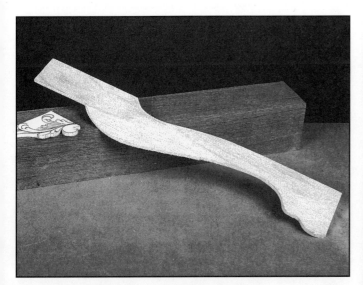

1 – Make a pattern of the front leg from masonite or plywood or simply use the paper pattern from the book.

2 – Trace the pattern of the leg on a piece of mahogany 3" square by 17" long.

4 – With a marking gauge, measure and lay out the mortises. Then cut the mortises.

3 – The pattern should be laid out on the stock as shown in the picture.

5 – With a bandsaw, start cutting out the pattern. The first cut begins at the back part of the leg, stopping before coming out of the wood.

6 – Now saw the front part of the leg up in the knee, again stopping before coming out of the wood.

7 – Repeat the same cut on the other side of the leg.

8 – Next cut the lower part of the leg starting at the knee and stopping before coming to the bottom of the toe.

9 – Repeat this process on the other side of the leg and you should have this result.

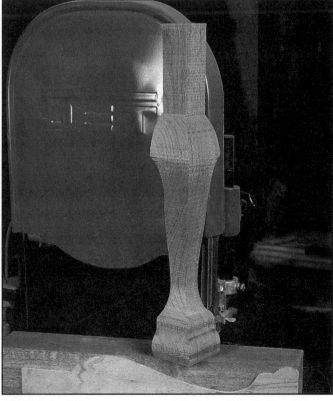

10 – Break off the waste stock and the leg will look like this.

11 – Find the center of the bottom of the foot.

12 – Next mark a circle approximately 2 inches in diameter.

13 – Here I am using an Easley vise. Begin shaping the lower part of the ankle.

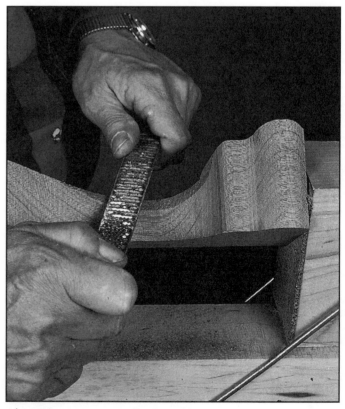

14 – With a coarse rasp, file the ankle into an octagonal shape.

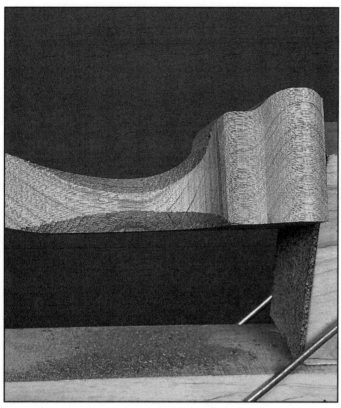

15 – The result is an octagon that can now be easily rounded into a circle.

16 – Round the ankle with a finer rasp.

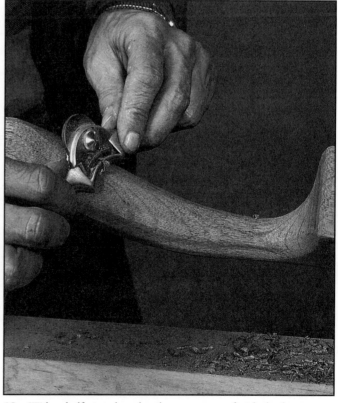

17 – With a spoke shave, begin to round the front part of the leg below the knee.

18 – With a half round spoke shave, you can finish the leg to a nicely rounded shape.

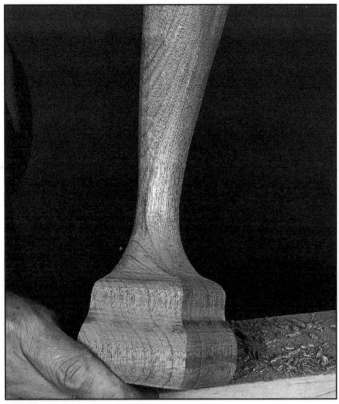

19 – Once the leg is shaped, you are ready to move on to the foot.

20 – Now with a half round wood rasp, begin shaping the middle part of the front foot.

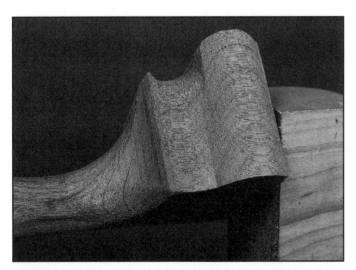

21 – When finished, the foot will look like this.

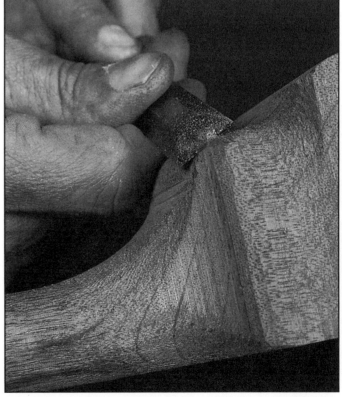

22 – With a flat chisel, continue to shape the foot by rounding the middle part of the front foot.

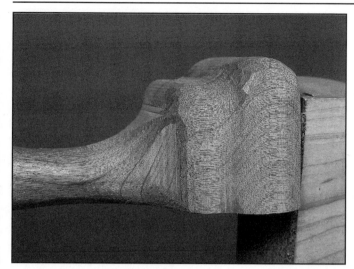

23 – Continue working on the foot until you are satisfied with the results.

24 – Repeat the rounding process on the outer areas of the foot.

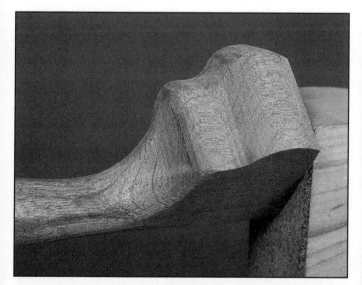

25 – The front of the foot should look approximately like this.

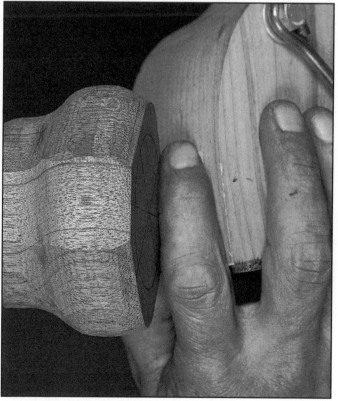

26 – This foot is now ready for some detail.

27 — Now mark a center line on the front of the foot.

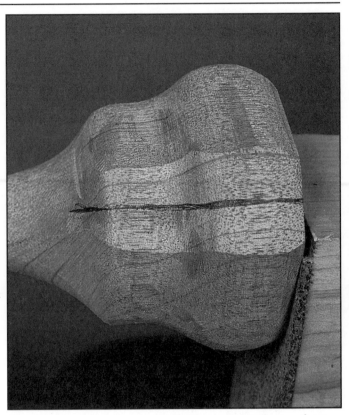

28 — This line will delineate the division between the two front toes.

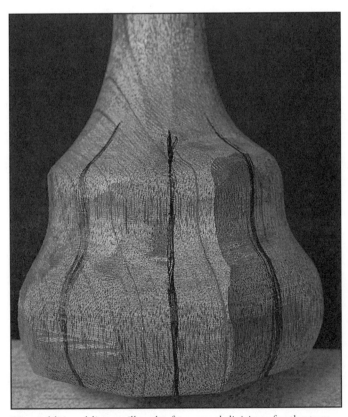

29 — Additional lines will make four equal divisions for the toes.

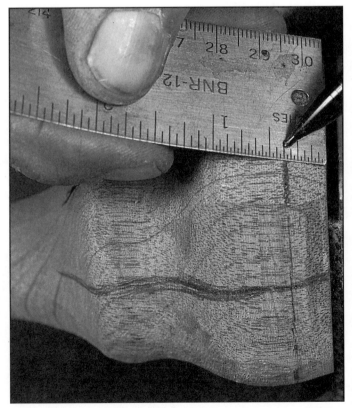

30 — Marking up ⅜", strike a line. This line will continue all the way around the bottom of the foot.

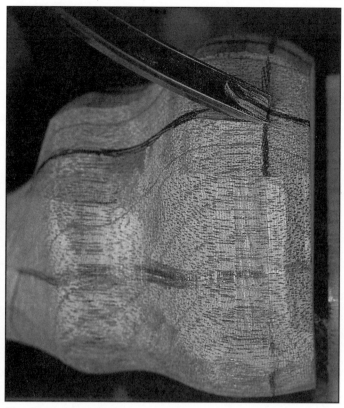

31 – Beginning with the two center toes, cut a groove down your center line with a v-gouge.

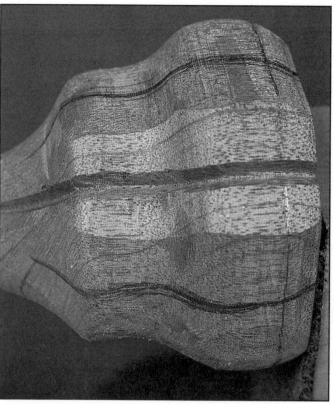

32 – The groove will make a separation between the two front toes.

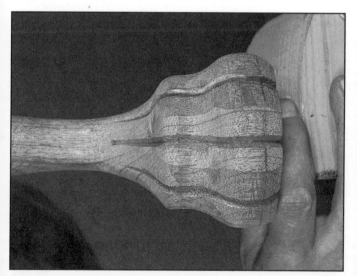

33 – Repeat this process on both sides of the center line, creating four distinct segments.

34 – With a flat chisel, begin rounding the segments into each other.

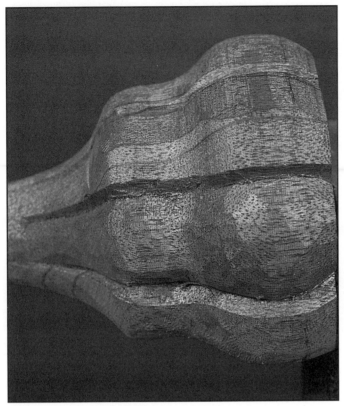

35 – Continue until the segments are well rounded.

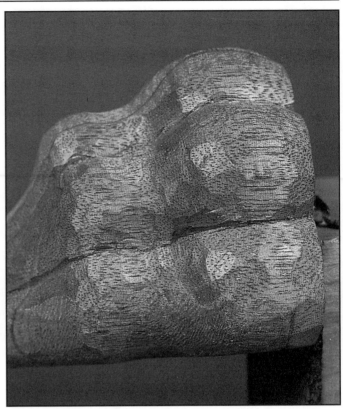

36 – The result will be four rounded lumps that will create four individual toes.

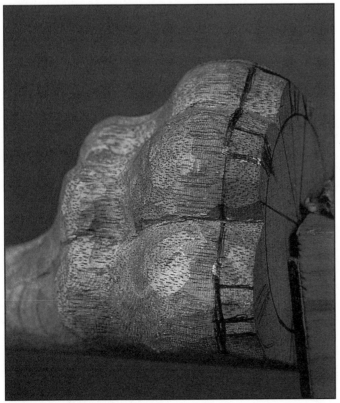

37 – Lay in the bottom of the toes and the claws. The ³⁄₈" line drawn previously will mark the bottom of the toes. From the center of each toe, mark in as shown in the photo to locate the claw.

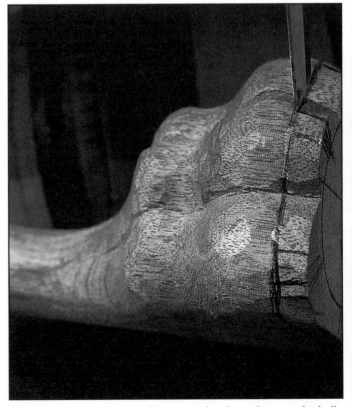

38 – Now remove the wood between the claws down to the ball. Starting with a flat chisel, set in along the line ³⁄₈" above the bottom of the foot.

39 – The resulting cut will look like this.

40 – You are now ready to finish shaping the bottoms of the toes. Begin with a v-gouge.

41 – Carefully round off the bottoms of the toes.

42 – Continue until the bottoms of the toes are nicely shaped.

43 – Now turn your attention to the back of the foot. Begin by tapering in with a flat chisel.

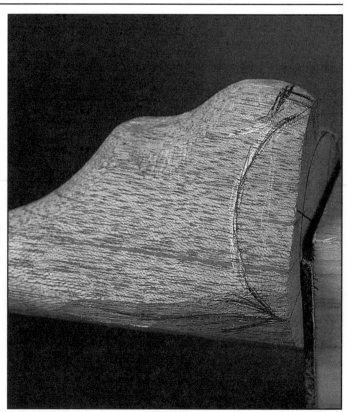

44 – Mark a half moon shape on the back of the foot on both sides.

45 – With a #5/25 or #5/30, set in along this line and remove the wood down to the circle drawn on the bottom of the foot.

46 – The resulting cut should look like this when viewed from the bottom of the foot.

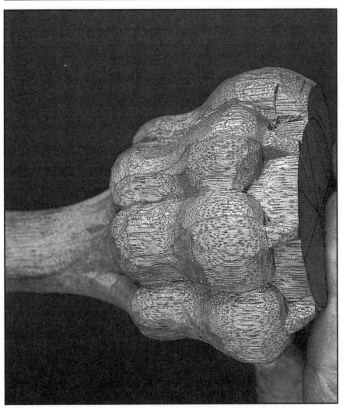

47 – The rough-shaped foot should look like this at this point.

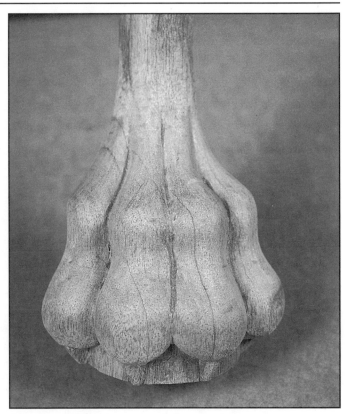

48 – The bald foot is now ready for some hair.

49 – To create the hair on this foot, we will need an assortment of chisels.

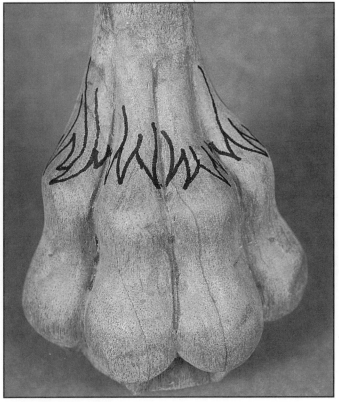

50 – Using the patterns in the book or by creating your own, mark out for the top layer of hair.

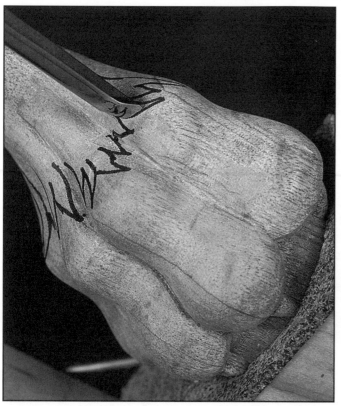

51 – Set in along these lines, with gouges that correspond to the shape of the line.

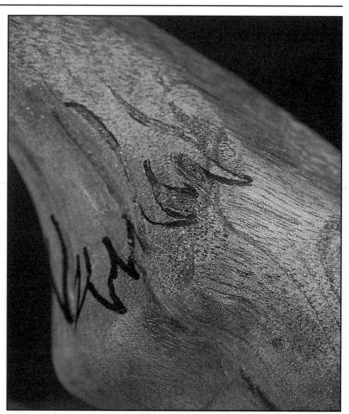

52 – Remove the wood up to the lines to give the illusion that they are sitting on the top of the toe.

53 – The resulting lines should look like the ones in this photograph.

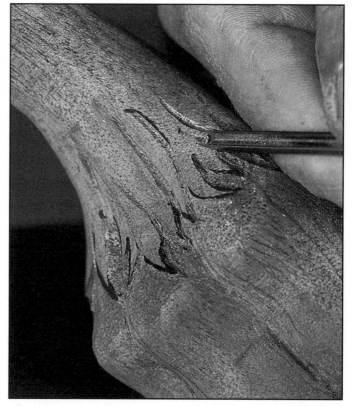

54 – With a #2 veiner, start to apply random cuts, which will give the illusion of hair.

55 – Continue to make random cuts, crossing the cuts occasionally to enhance the illusion.

56 – Repeat the process along the top grouping of hairs.

57 – Now draw the elements for the lower knuckles and repeat the process once again.

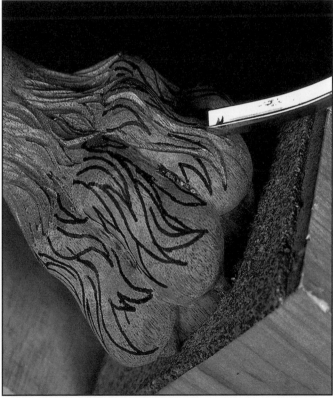

58 – A v-gouge is helpful in delineating the various hair elements.

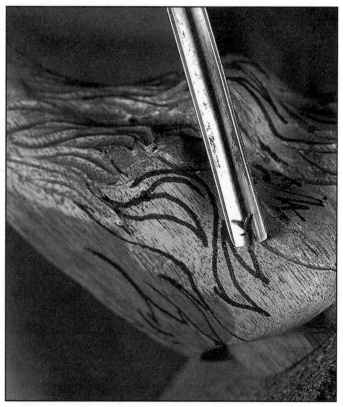

59 – Continue working until you reach the bottom of the toe.

60 – The cuts that you've made to this point should look like this.

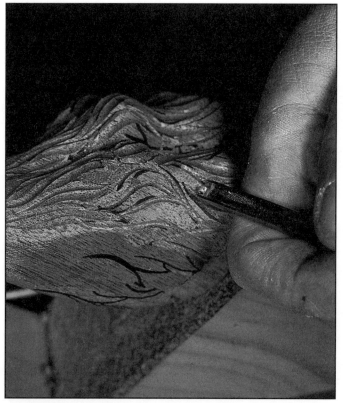

61 – With various gouges, including small 9's and veiners, begin accentuating the flow of the hair.

62 – Care should be taken to make this area as realistic as possible.

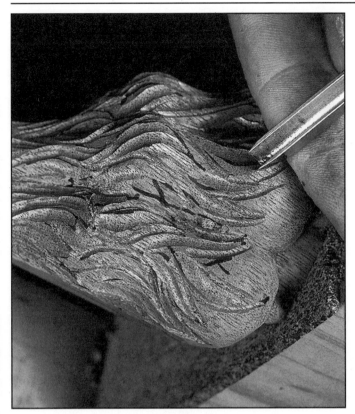

63 — Continue making cuts to create the illusion of hair.

64 — Once the hair on the front of the foot is completed to your satisfaction, you are ready to begin carving the hair on the back of the foot.

65 — Begin by drawing a random flow of tufts using the drawing in the book as a guide.

66 — Set in along these lines.

67 – Remove the wood in between these locks down to the surface of the ball.

68 – These first cuts should look like this.

69 – Now try to make the hairs appear as if they are laying on top of each other. To do this, some undercutting is necessary.

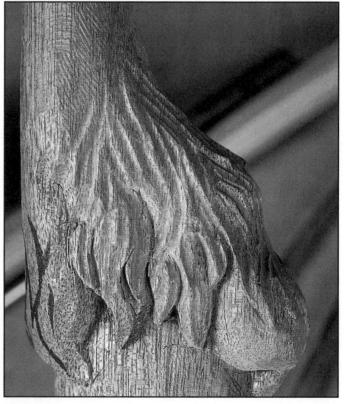

70 – Again, the hair should look as realistic as possible.

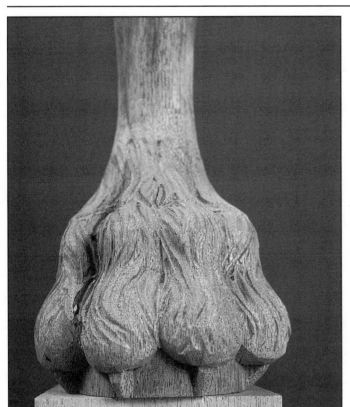

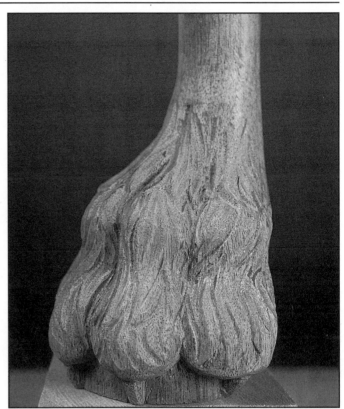

71–76 – Series of photos of the finished foot from different angles

72

73

74

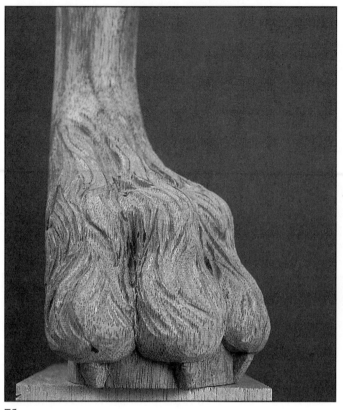

75

76

CHAPTER 14

Detailing the Knee Returns

1 – To finish the shaping of the top part of the knee, apply the knee returns by gluing and clamping them to the chair.

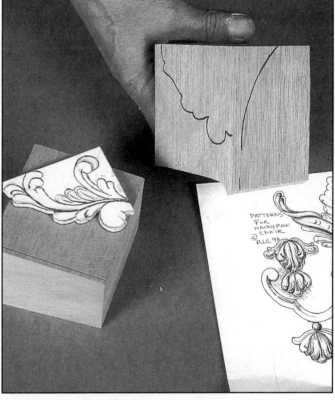

2 – Using the pattern supplied in the book and marking the shape of the inside of the knee on the top of the block, cut out on a bandsaw.

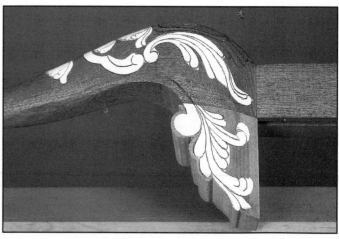

4 – Copy the patterns for the carvings and apply them to the leg with rubber cement.

3 – Now it can be glued to the leg, making sure it is even with the bottom of the mortise so that when the seat rails are joined, everything fits tightly.

5 – Begin setting in as we have done before, using the appropriately shaped gouges.

6 – Carefully remove the paper patterns from the knee return. Any excess rubber cement left on the wood can be rubbed away with your fingers.

7 – With the paper patterns removed, this is the result.

8 – Remove the background area around the carved elements.

9 – Continue to work on the carved elements.

10 – Patience in this area will give you excellent results.

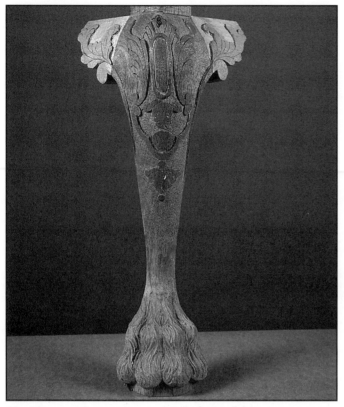

11 – The carved areas are now ready for modeling.

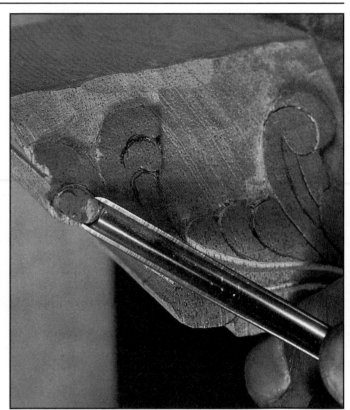

12 – Create the modeling using appropriate gouges, mostly 8's and 9's.

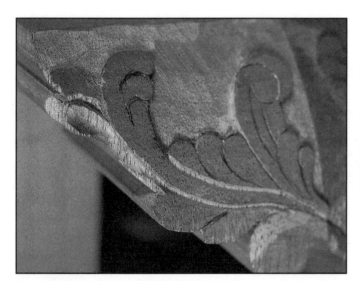

13 – The resulting gouge cut will look like this.

14–18 – This series of photos shows the modeling of this area.

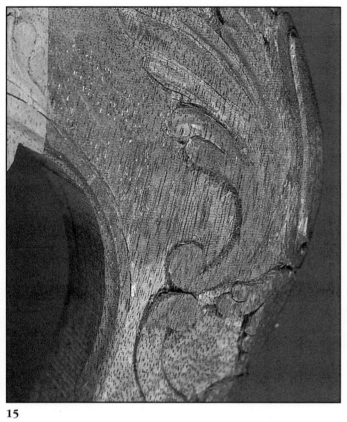

15

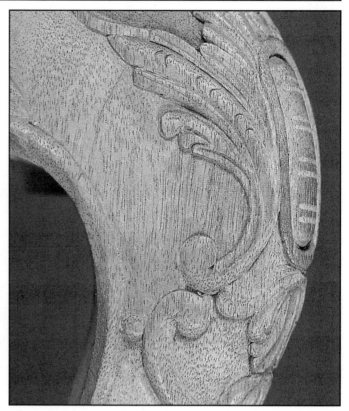

16

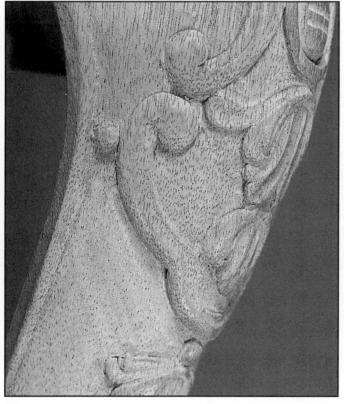

17

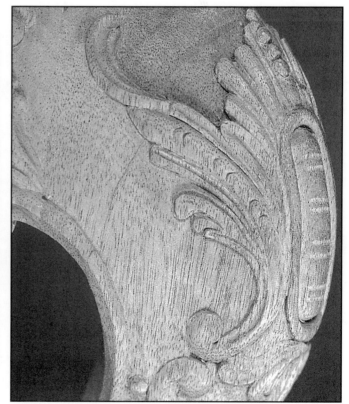

18

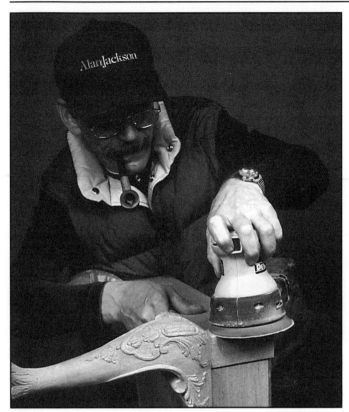

19 – This photo, though it shows a step further along in the process of assembling the chair, gives you a good look at the finished knee return.

CHAPTER 15

Creating the Seat Rails

2 – Laying out for the tenons is a critical step. The rear tennon on the side rails results in compound cuts. Refer to the plan drawings to make accurate cuts.

1 – After you have completed all the carving, turn your attention to the side seat rails.

3 – To do this, I use special jigs, one for the left and one for the right, that I created for the bandsaw.

4 – With the seat rail clamped to the jig, begin sawing the faces of the tenons.

5 – Continue sawing until the length of the tenons is completed.

6 – With a handsaw, carefully cut the shoulders.

7 – The result is an angled tennon for the back leg. Note that the front tenon on the side seat rail is not angled.

8 – With a ¼" round over bit, apply the molding to the top of the seat rail.

9 – With a reduced bearing and setting the bit to ³⁄₃₂, this will create two fillets on the bead.

10 – Begin routing.

11 – The resulting routing will look like this.

12 – With a sacked head dado set, cut a rabbet in the top of the seat rail to hold the seat frame.

13 – With the measurements given in the book marked onto the seat rail, begin cutting the rabbet.

14 – This step needs to be repeated for the front seat rail and the two other sides.

CHAPTER 16

Detailing the Front Seat Rail
Gadrooning

1 – Between the two front legs and the bottom of the front seat rail is another gadroon element. To make this, start with a piece of mahogany ⅝" thick and slightly longer than the opening between the knee blocks.

2 – With a ½" round over bit placed in a router table, begin rounding over the front edge.

3 – Continue rounding over the front edge.

4 – The result will look like this.

5 – Find the center by measuring the length of the board and dividing it in half.

6 – Divide each side into 11 equal segments.

7 – Using the drawing from the book, lay out for your gadrooning.

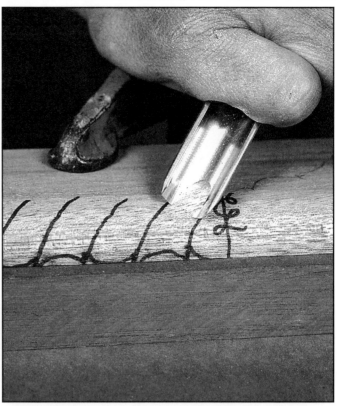

8 – Carve this gadrooning with a slightly different method than that used earlier. Using a #9/15, begin to carve in all the concave segments.

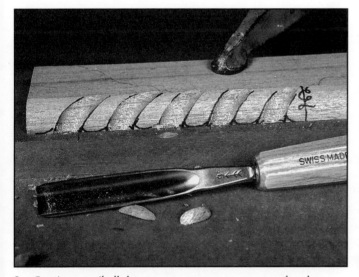

9 – Continue until all the concave segments are completed.

10 – Turning over the board, use the same gouge to carve in from the front. Taper these cuts in from the back as shown in the photo.

11 – Continue carving these secondary cuts.

12 – The end result will look like this.

13 – Now using a #2 gouge, round over the convex elements into the concave elements.

14 – The result is a piece of wood that appears to be twisting.

15 – Now at this point, you may want to sand these areas, followed by some Scotch Brite.

16 – The result should look like a smooth, wavy piece of wood.

17 – Redraw the dividing lines between the segments and carve them out with a v-gouge.

18 – Finish rounding the convex elements using the same #2 gouge as earlier.

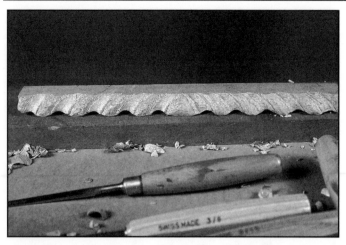

19 – Repeat the procession on both sides of the center, and this is the result.

CHAPTER 17

Assembling the Chair

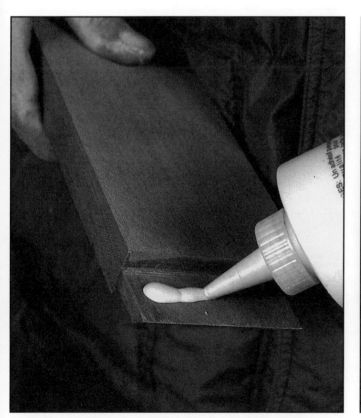

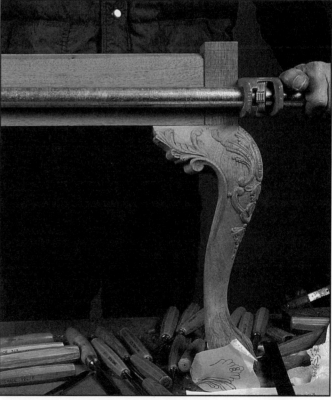

1 – Now we can begin assembling the chair. Starting with the front rail, apply the glue to the tenons.

2 – With the tenons placed into the mortises, apply clamp pressure, allowing the piece to sit overnight. I always wait until the piece is dry to remove the excess glue with a scraper.

3 – With the clamps still in place, mark the areas for the pins.

4 – Use a ¼" drill bit to drill through the front legs and tenon.

5 – This hole will serve as an insertion point for a pin.

6 – Make some ¼" pegs from some scrap material.

7 – Once they have been whittled into shape, they can be driven into the holes.

8 – Repeat this process for the side rails.

9 – Note that the tenon on the side rail comes through the back leg. This will be sawn off later.

10 – Now, apply clamps to both sides.

11 – With a handsaw, trim off the top of the leg that sticks above the seat rail.

12 – Once that has been completed, this part of the leg needs to be rabbetted out to receive the seat frame.

13 – You can begin sanding the chair after the glue has dried. Continue sanding the chair until all tool marks have been sanded away.

14 – With the same round over bit in the router as you used on the front and side rails, apply the molding to the top front legs.

CHAPTER 18

Staining and Finishing

1 – Now you are ready to stain and finish the chair. Because finishing can be such a personal matter, the following will be recommendations only.

2 – I prefer to use water-based stains. Using a combination of various shades, I have created a nice tone of brown mahogany, which can be applied with either a brush or a rag.

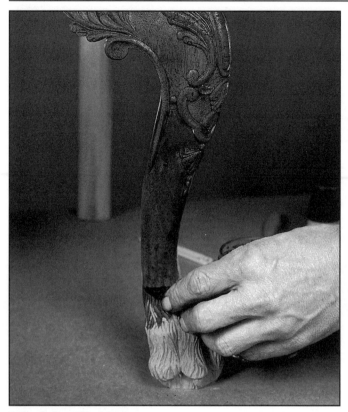

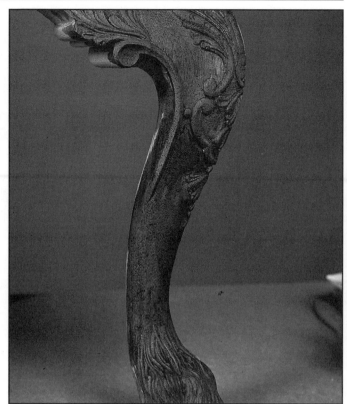

3–7 – Series of staining.

4

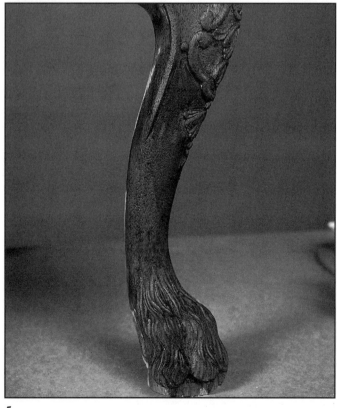

5

6

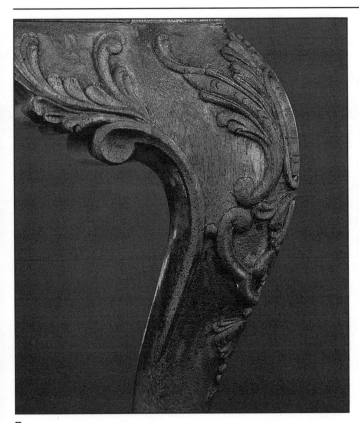

7

8 – Because of the complex nature of Chippendale chairs, I prefer to use an HVLP spray system to coat the piece with shellac. If you opt to use this method, be sure to rub the piece down between coats with either steel wool or Scotch Brite.

18th Century Plans

Reproduction Furniture in
Authentic Measured Drawings

By Ron Clarkson

Ron Clarkson has received many requests for full size measured drawings
of the many pieces he has made over the years.

Currently, you can order the following from your favorite bookstore or
woodworking supply house. If you can't find them locally you may order
directly from the publisher below. Please send us your name and address if
you wish to be added to the mailing list for future patterns.

PieCrust Tea Table
1 sheet, 18 inches by 25 inches

Contains full details of the table top and edging as well the unique bird-
cage pedestal upon which the table sits. The table rotates on an open
bird-cage. The pedestal is carved with designs of acanthus leaves, ribbons
and flowers and rests on 3 carved cabriole legs ending in a classic ball and
claw foot. $15.00

Chippendale Chairs
Please see the Measured Drawings section for reduced views of these.

Chair #1 - Ball and Claw with Acanthus Detail
2 sheets, 24 inches by 36 inches

A fully carved back starting with a crestrail combining cabison, acanthus
and bell flower carving. Flowing into a strap work pierced backsplat,
having a central carved element. Two fully carved rear legs and two fully
carved acanthus front legs. Terminating in ball and claw feet. $15.00

Chair #2 - Hairy Paw Foot
2 sheets, 24 inches by 36

An acanthus and C scroll carved chair, flowing into a pierced carved
Gothic Splat and terminating with a gadrooned carved shoe. A plain front
skirt and gadrooned apron flanked by cabisoned and acanthus carved legs,
ending in articulated hairy paw feet. $15.00

Chair #3 - Ball and Claw with Shell Detail
2 sheets, 24 inches by 36 inches

A fully carved crestrail with two shell carved ears, flowing into a entral
carved shell. A fully pierced and scrolled backsplat with two cabriole front
legs with shells on the knees, ending in a ball and claw foot. $15.00

Measured Drawings
Fox Chapel Publishing
Box 7948
Lancaster, Pa 17604
1-800-457-9112

GLOSSARY

Acanthus leaf – A naturalistic form of ornament of classic derrivation.

Burnishing tool – A short round or oval-shaped rod of case-hardened steel, mounted and used to turn the sharpened edge of a steel woodscraper blade.

Champher/bevel – A 45-degree angle planed or chiseled on the edge of any surface.

Chippendale – Referes to the style originated by Thomas Chippendale, an English cabinetmaker, one of the four most famous designers of furniture of the 18th century.

Dado head – A combination of dado saw blades, or of two dado saw blades and one or more chipper blades, sometimes called spaced blades.

Gadroon – A carved molding, also known as nulling, consisting of short flutes and reeds which are sloped.

Gouge – A chisel having a blade the cutting edge of which is "U" shaped or in the form of a semi-circle.

Knee – The upper part of a cabriole leg which swells outward from the frame.

Low relief – A modeled carving on which the background is lowered not more than an eighth of an inch.

Macaroni – A term sometimes applied to a wood carving chisel whose cutting edges are formed into a squared "U" shape.

Mallet – A hammer of wood or hard rubber or some other material. It has a barrel shaped head and is used for driving tools such as chisels into wood.

Marking gauge – A tool that consists of a square wooden bar usually eight inches long on which a wooden head slides. It is used to mark lines parallel to the edges or sides of boards.

Masonite – A fiber board made from steam exploded wood fibers.

Mortise and tennon – A joint commonly used in woodworking, consisting of a rectangular cavity cut into a piece of wood (mortise) and an end sticking out from a shoulder at the end of another piece of wood (tennon) that fit together.

Rabbit – A groove or step cut on the edge of a board.

Relief carving – A form of ornament in which the figure is put into relief by lowering the background and also shaping the design itself.

Shellac – A finish material made from processed lac mixed with alcohol. Lac is a resinous substance secreted by an insect to cover its eggs.

Splat – The vertical central member in a chair back.

Spoke shave – A two-handled tool used to plane sticks of wood into cylindrical shapes.

MUSEUMS

Metropolitan Museum of Art
6626 Metropolitan Avenue
Flushing, NY 11379
(718) 326–7050

Museum of Fine Arts
465 Huntington Avenue
Boston, MA 02115
(617) 267–9300

Philadelphia Museum of Fine Art
25th and Benjamin Franklin Parkway
Philadelphia, PA 19104
(215) 763–8100

Winterthur Museum
Route 52
Winterthur, DE 19735
(302) 888–4600

Wadsworth Antheneum
600 Main Street
Hartford, CT 06130
(860) 278–2670

Historical Society of Pennsylvania
1300 Locust Street
Philadelphia, PA 19107
(215) 732–6200

Historic Deerfield, Inc.
321 Main Street
Deerfield, MA 01342
(413) 774–5581

The Yale University Art Gallery
1111 Chapel Street
New Haven, CT 06510
(203) 432–0600

The Carnegie Museum of Art
4400 Forbes Avenue
Pittsburgh, PA 15213
(412) 622–3131

Colonial Williamsburg
Duke of Gloucester Street
Williamsburg, VA 23185
(804) 229–2141

The Charleston Museum
360 Meeting Street
Charleston, SC 29403
(803) 722–2996

The National Trust for Historic Preservation
House Museums
Located throughout the United States

The Museum of Art
Rhode Island School of Design
2 College Street
Providence, RI 02903
(401) 454–6500

The Diplomatic Reception Rooms
State Department
2201 C Street NW
Washington, D.C. 20520
(202) 647–5268

The Los Angeles County Museum of Art
5905 Wilshire Boulevard
Los Angeles, CA 90036
(213) 857–6000

The Bayou Bend Collection of Arts
1 Westcott Street
Houston, TX 77007
(713) 520–2600

The Maryland Historical Society
201 West Monument Street
Baltimore, MD 21201
(410) 685–3750

The Henry Ford Museum and The Greenfield Village
20900 Oakwood Boulevard
Dearborn, Michigan 48124
(313) 271–1620

The Museum of Early Southern Decorative Arts (MESDA)
924 South Main Street
Winston-Salem, NC 27104
(910) 721–7360

SUGGESTED READING

The Gentleman & Cabinet-Maker's Director, Thomas Chippendale, third edition. Reprint. Dover Publications, 1966.

American Furniture: Seventeenth, Eighteenth and Nineteenth Century Styles, Helen Comstock. New York, The Viking Press, New York, 1962.

American Furniture, Queen Anne and Chippendale Periods in the Henry Francis du Pont Winterthur Museum, Joseph Downs. Macmillan Co., New York, 1952.

The Life and Works of Thomas Chippendale, Volume 2, Christopher Gilbert. Macmillan Co., 1978.

A Winterthur Guide to American Chippendale Furniture, Charles F. Hummel. Crown Publishers, New York, 1976.

Furniture Treasury, Wallace Nutting. Three volumes. Reprint. Macmillan Co., New York, 1954.

American Antiques from Isreal Sach Collection. Seven volumes. Highland House Publishers, Washington, D.C., 1950.

American Furniture in the Metropolitan Museum of Art, Late Colonial Period, Morrison H. Heckscher. Random House.

Centuries and Styles of the American Chair: 1640–1970, Robert Bishop. E.P. Dutton and Co., New York, 1972.

The Philadelphia Chair: 1685–1785, Joseph K. Kindig III. The Historical Society of York County, Harrisburg, Pa.

American Chairs: Queen Anne and Chippendale. Alfred A. Knopf, New York, 1972.

With Hammer in Hand: The Dominy Craftsmen of East Hampton. The University Press of Virginia, Charlottesville, 1968.

Blue Book: Philadelphia Furniture, William MacPherson Horner, Jr. Reprint. Highland House Publishers, Washington, D.C.

Eighteenth-Century American Arts: The M. and M. Karolik Collection. Cambridge Harvard University Press for the Museum of Fine Arts, Boston, 1941.

ABOUT THE AUTHOR

When the prototype for one of Ron Clarkson's furniture reproductions sold for $3.6 million at Sotheby's in New York last January, Ron wasn't the least bit surprised.

"It was a gorgeous piece," he said. "That desk was a beautiful example of the craftsmanship of furniture makers from the 18th century."

Made from mahogany and adorned with intricate hand-carved shells, "that desk" is a Newport block-front knee-hole desk, 1765–1785, originally made by Edmund Townsend. Ron, who crafts furniture reproductions in his Chestertown, Maryland, studio, was commissioned by the owners to make a reproduction of the piece before it went on the auction block in New York.

"Making any kind of a reproduction is a challenge," Ron said about his work. "It takes a lot of research to get the feel of the piece and to make an accurate reproduction."

Ron first became interested in furniture reproduction more than 25 years ago when he started doing furniture refinishing and repairs for a small shop in his hometown of Chestertown, Maryland. Gradually, his interests focused in on reproductions of furniture from 18th century America, such as Queen Anne, Chippendale and Newport style furniture.

"I like being able to bring back a form of artistry that I feel has been missing," Ron said. "The furniture makers who were creating chairs and tables and such back in the 18th century were doing so on a commercial level, yet still managed to put artistry and elegance first in their work."

Today, Ron finishes eight to ten reproductions each year. He has made chairs, cabinets, "pie-crust" tables, beds and more, and his pieces have been purchased by collectors as far away from his studio in Chestertown as Washington, Florida, Michigan and England. He has created pieces for Mount Vernon and the Queenstown Court House in Maryland. In addition to carving, Ron also finds time to give lectures and teach classes about antique restoration and reproduction.

Making Classic Chairs: A Craftsman's Chippendale Reference. is Ron's first book for Fox Chapel Publishing. He has also written two other books on reproductions: *Making Classic Carved Furniture: The Queen Anne Stool* and *Classic Carved Furniture: Making a Piecrust Tea Table.*

TOPICAL INDEX

NEW AND RECENT BOOK TITLES...
...from the experts!

Making Classic Chairs:
A Craftsman's Chippendale Reference
Ron Clarkson & Tom Heller

188 pp. softcover
1-56523-081-7 $24.95

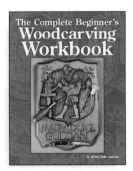

Complete Beginner's Woodcarving Workbook
Mary Duke Guldan

Softcover, 56 pages, 8.5 x 11
1-56523-085-X $9.95

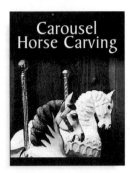

Carousel Horse Carving:
An Instructional Workbook in 1/3 scale
Ken Hughes

Perfect bound, color and black and white, how-to information, tool lists, full size pattern included.
1-56523-072-8 $24.95

East Weekend Carving Projects
Tina Toney

56 pp. perfect bound, color and black and white, step-by-step carving and painting demonstrations patterns.
1-56523-084-1 $12.95

Santas and Snowmen:
Carving for Christmas
Tina Toney

56 pp. softcover, Full color.
1-56523-083-3 $12.95

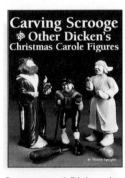

Carving Scrooge and Dickens's "A Christmas Carol"
(plus the Olde London Towne scene)
Vince Squeglia

56 pp. 10 complete patterns, full color gallery included.
1-56523-082-5 $12.95

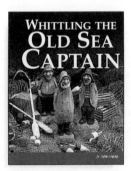

Whittling the Old Sea Captain
Mike Shipley

48 pp. perfect bound, color and black and white. Includes step-by-step carving & painting demonstrations, patterns, color photos of the finished captain crew.
1-56523-075-2 $12.95

Free Form Chip Carving
Carol A. Ponte

48 pp. softcover
1-56523-080-9 $7.95

Santa Carving With Myron Bowman

56 pp. perfect bound, color and black and white. Includes step-by-step carving and painting demonstrations, 11 patterns, color photos of finished Santas.
1-56523-076-0 $12.95

ox Chapel Publishing Co., Inc.
PO Box 7948
Lancaster, PA 17604-7948